M000307101

What a really useful re
book ... and I'm looking
at Christmas is preached once more. As I read through it, I found
that ideas for carol service talks just kept leaping off its pages.

Rico Tice
co-author of Christianity Explored
Associate Minister at All Souls Church
Langham Place, London

One of the deepest and most fulfilling joys one could experience
on earth is that of drinking from the deep well of God's truth.
But most Christians believe that such pursuits are reserved for
those who have been initiated to the intricacies of theological
study. In this book we see the profound truths of the incarnation
presented in a way that makes the Bible and its truth come alive.
And, best of all, it is presented in an engaging style that makes it
accessible to ordinary laypersons.

Ajith Fernando
Teaching Director, Youth for Christ, Sri Lanka

Tragically, on his birthday, the profound significance of why Jesus
came to earth tends to get lost in the crush of the celebration.
But now, thanks to Peter Mead, the story of the most significant
birth in history has been brought back to its proper place in this
compelling read. *Pleased To Dwell* traces the promised hope of
his arrival from the prophetic voices of the Old Testament to
the actual event and its transforming relevance to our lives today.
This book is perfect food for the heart for all of us who long for
a richer understanding of the birth of The King!

Joseph M. Stowell
President, Cornerstone University, Grand Rapids, Michigan

Peter Mead offers a wonderful presentation of Jesus that brings
together more of the Bible than you'll find anywhere else. It's
a tour de force in tracing themes of Christ coming from heaven
to humanity. It's also a lively and compelling read. Peter leads

readers into the Bible with a crisp clarity that brings out Old and New Testament connections that have always been there. If you'd like to know Jesus better you must read this book!

Ronald N. Frost
Pastoral Care Consultant, Barnabas International, and Mentor, Cor Deo, Chippenham, England

Through a clear and accessible explanation of the profound miracle of the incarnation, Peter Mead provides not only an illuminating Bible overview but a call to trust the Lord Jesus who is central to God's purposes. An ideal introduction to a profound theme – and a great Christmas present!

Jonathan Lamb
CEO and minister-at-large for Keswick Ministries, and IFES Vice President

'God so loved the world, that he gave his only Son' – this is the greatest love story ever told. This wonderful book tells the awesome story of God giving his Son in a way that is thoroughly biblical and deeply engaging. Peter Mead masterfully handles sweeping vistas while paying close attention to textual details, all with an engaging enthusiasm. Whether you are exploring the claims of Christianity for the first time, a new believer seeking to understand the Bible better, or a seasoned Christian wanting to reinvigorate your love for Christ, this book is a must read. It is also perfect if you are a preacher looking to present the "big picture" of the gospel or planning a Christmas preaching series. I wholeheartedly recommend *Pleased to Dwell*, and I am sure that many will love the Savior more as a result of reading this!

Alexander Strauch
Author of Biblical Eldership, conference speaker and elder at Littleton Bible Chapel, Denver, Colorado

In this helpful book Peter Mead tells the big story of the incarnation from the Old to the New Testament. He tells the story as a story helping the reader to appreciate the various scriptures in their own right and to see how magnificently God planned this great event. The book is written with clarity and freshness and flows in a way that makes reading enjoyable as well as a blessing. It is a work of biblical theology from a preacher who appreciates the need to communicate biblical truth in an engaging way. It treats the incarnation with reverence while at the same time demonstrating the practical importance of this doctrine in the life of every Christian. This book could be read anytime but would be great tool for personal spiritual preparation for Christmas and could form the basis of a Christmas time teaching series. I recommend it highly.

Stephen McQuoid
General Director of Gospel Literature Outreach, Motherwell,
Scotland

A bright and breezy (and therefore very readable) sprint through the Bible's story of Jesus, from Genesis to Revelation. With brief and accessible chapters, it would make an ideal Quiet Times book for the run up to Christmas, as well as a perfect introduction to these foundational truths for a young believer. Thoroughly recommended.

Mark Meynell
European Director of Langham Preaching and author of Cross-
Examined, IVP.

I have a confession to make... I don't like Christmas! At least by Christmas I mean the tinsel and the trimmings that fill our shops earlier and earlier every year. But in this easily accessible and encouraging book, Peter Mead shows us that the true heart of Christmas, the incarnation, is something to rejoice in every day of the year. This book is for life and not just for Christmas!

Michael Ots
Evangelist, author of *What Kind of God?*
Bournemouth, England

What unites the Scriptures? A plan of salvation? A pattern of redemption? Promises of abstract blessings? Peter Mead answers with heart-warming clarity: a Person. It's the Person of Christ who is communicated on every page – a Person who longs to be known personally. *Pleased to Dwell* walks us through the Bible to see its central Character afresh and to rejoice in His desire to draw near. This book will surprise, teach, encourage and gladden you as you encounter Jesus in both Old and New Testaments.

Glen Scrivener
Evangelist and author of *3-2-1*.
Eastbourne, England

PLEASED
TO
DWELL

A Biblical Introduction to the Incarnation

PETER MEAD

CHRISTIAN
FOCUS

Peter Mead is director of *Cor Deo*, a mentored ministry training programme based in Chippenham, England. He is on the leadership team of a church plant and leads the Bible Teachers & Preachers Networks at the European Leadership Forum. He studied at Multnomah Biblical Seminary and received his Doctor of Ministry degree from Gordon-Conwell Theological Seminary. Peter is married to Melanie and they have five children.

Copyright © Peter Mead 2014

paperback ISBN 978-1-78191-426-7
epub ISBN 978-1-78191-507-3
Mobi ISBN 978-1-78191-511-0
10 9 8 7 6 5 4 3 2 1

Printed in 2014
by
Christian Focus Publications Ltd.,
Geanies House, Fearn, Ross-shire,
IV20 1TW, Scotland, UK.

www.christianfocus.com

Cover design by Daniel van Straaten

Printed by
Bell and Bain, Glasgow

CONTENTS

Acknowledgments

In recent years I have had the privilege of studying the Bible and theology in the context of Cor Deo – a small mentoring programme that exists to multiply ministry that shares God's heart. Being with people who have a passion to know and love a loving God is a real delight. I must especially thank Ron Frost for partnering in this ministry. I have learned so much from Ron and his delight in the God who reveals Himself in His Word. I am thankful to be able to work alongside David Searight and Mike Chalmers. I thank God for each participant in the full-time programme – it really is a joy to learn, serve and grow together.

I must also mention Mike Reeves, whose encouragement and friendship have made a real difference to this project. It has been great to work with the folks at Christian Focus. But I can't finish without expressing my gratitude to God for Melanie, a wife whose heart values reflect His in so many ways. Her impact on my life and our children's lives cannot be measured.

Foreword

I've always loved Christmas. It's always seemed so cheery and snug, so homely and happy. And that hasn't gone away for me as a Christian. The more I know Christ, the more I enjoy celebrating his birth. Jesus makes the joy of Christmas go *deeper*. So in December I always try to find a good book or two about Jesus, something that wipes the eyes to see him more clearly, something that says 'O come, let us adore him!'

This is just that sort of book. Really it is a small library of stories that work together to increase your wonder at what happened on that first Christmas. It would be a good read at any time of year, but it works especially well as an

Advent book. And like Advent, it brims with a sense of gathering excitement: starting in the Old Testament and moving through history, the anticipation heightens and each chapter seems more moving than the last.

Anyone who has met Peter Mead will know that there is nothing stiff or dry about him. He is a man warmed and delighted by God, a man who wants to share the satisfaction he finds in Christ. And that is just what you find here: a book groaning with bible insights from Old and New Testaments, all drawing you to marvel and worship. Peter wears his scholarship lightly, but deftly draws thread after thread of Scripture together, making you marvel at the richness of God's word, the intricacy and kindness of his plans, and the dazzling glory of Christ.

Here, then, is a chance to enter more deeply into the very joy of heaven itself. After all, Christ the everlasting Lord is, as Charles Wesley put it, the one '*by highest heaven adored*'. Here is what angels long to look into. Here is what thrills the heart of the Father.

Michael Reeves

Introduction

I enjoyed my first job, most of the time. We had just been married a few weeks and moved back to England from the U.S.A. I had been looking for a job to pay the bills, but did not want one that would consume all my time and energy. I ended up selling memberships for a leading breakdown service! No salary, commission only. No yellow of our competitor, orange only.

I did this job for almost two years, before we packed up and moved back across the ocean so that I could return to Bible school. Two summers. Motorists heading off on holiday, beautiful weather, and for the most part, decent sales. And two winters. Standing in the freezing temperatures and seemingly endless rain. Strangely though, December was always my best month!

Despite the rain and the lack of daylight, December was a special time. Lots of people frantically preparing for holiday season, and somehow, lots of people willing to spend even more money on breakdown coverage. Perhaps it was the threat of being stranded in appalling weather, or perhaps it was my happy mood.

Maybe I should be embarrassed to admit it, but I quite enjoyed standing in the entrance to a supermarket, or in the centre of Bristol, with the Christmas music blasting out as a constant pagan soundtrack for the season. *When the snowman brings the snow ... Christmas time, mistletoe and wine ... it's the season for love and understanding, Merry Christmas, everyone! ... in our world of plenty, we can spread a smile of joy ... Oh I wish it could be Christmas every day.*

Now that is the dream of every child. Christmas every day! And what is the big deal for many children today? Presents! I suppose it sounds so materialistic, so selfish, when we stop to evaluate the content of a commercialised Christmas.

But here is a thought to ponder. Christianity is a faith with Christmas in its DNA. Every day is shot through with the reality that heaven has broken into the world, and now everything is different.

Jonathan Edwards described heaven as a world of love. Heaven is where the Father delights in the Son and lovingly glorifies Him. The Son reciprocates and praises the Father with pure love. The Spirit bonds Father and Son in a perfect community of steadfast love and faithfulness. And the Bible tells us that heaven has broken into our world and invited us into that communion!

At the centre of heaven is Christ, lovingly adored as the forever Lord of all. At the centre of Christmas is Christ, frail and cradled in the tender arms of a young mother. How can the two be put together? Heavenly glory and human frailty? That is the real wonder of Christmas:

> Christ by highest heav'n adored,
> Christ the everlasting Lord,
> Late in time behold him come,
> Offspring of a virgin's womb.
> Veiled in flesh the Godhead see,
> Hail the incarnate deity,
> Pleased as man with man to dwell,
> Jesus our Immanuel
> Hark! The herald angels sing
> 'Glory to the newborn King!'[1]

This book is a biblical introduction to Christmas. It is an invitation to ponder a God who was pleased to dwell with us! The goal is not to rehearse the theological terminology of the heresies that have been offered in discussing the person of Christ or the hypostatic union. He is fully God, fully man, and fully one. The goal in this book is to have our hearts stirred by the Bible itself. In fact, if this book motivates you to put it down and pick up the Bible instead, I would consider that a success! The best way to get to know God is to chase Him through the Bible as you devour it cover to cover like a good book (which it is!).

So let's head off together into part one for a quick jog through the Old Testament to trace some of the themes that converge on that night when Mary gave birth to Jesus. There is the great sin problem, but also the wonder of

---

1.   Charles Wesley, 'Hark the Herald Angels Sing.' 1739.

God's promised provision in the seed of the woman who would crush the head of the serpent.

Part two slows down in the first two chapters of Matthew's Gospel. His account of that first Christmas is such a compelling presentation of prophecy fulfilled and the great plan of promise coming to fruition.

Part three then considers Luke's very different but fully complementary account of the birth of Christ. Luke's careful research of the eyewitnesses and diligent demonstration of the truthfulness of his account are a delight to ponder.

Part four concludes the book by considering a handful of other New Testament passages that speak of the coming of Christ to the earth.

I hope this brief book might stir in others the delight that writing it has stirred in me. Veiled in flesh ... Godhead see ... incarnate deity!

PART ONE:

The Anointed Deliverer

Old Testament Anticipation

I will put enmity between you and the woman,
and between your offspring and her offspring;
he shall bruise your head,
and you shall bruise his heel.
— Genesis 3:15 —

In the midst of the dirge of gloom and rebuke came
God's surprising word of prophetic hope.
A divinely instigated hostility. ... He would deliver
a lethal blow to the head of Satan, while the best the
serpent would be able or even permitted to do would
be to nip the heel of this male descendant.[1]
— Walter Kaiser —

---

1.   Walter Kaiser, *The Promise Plan of God* (Grand Rapids: Zondervan, 2008), p. 43.

1

The Person of Promise

Genesis 3:15

Everything around us whispers a double message to our hearts. On the one hand we hear the hints of original perfection: the stunning sunset, the intricate leaf, the refreshing breeze and the singing birds. At the same time we cannot miss the despairing groans of a broken creation: parched land in famine, ravaged forests, natural disaster and overwhelming death.

THE GREAT DESIGN

In the beginning God created everything, and it was good. The stage was set, the cast of creation swam and flew and grazed. And the main character, the pinnacle of creation, came last. The human. Adam. Actually, Adam and Eve. The pinnacle of creation was not man alone, for that was not good; it was male and female humanity, united yet diverse, made in the image of the God who spoke it all into being.

'Let us make man in our image.' Accidental plural? 'Royal we?' Not at all. The clues in Genesis 1 point to a plurality in the unity of God. The language nudges us towards a relational understanding of the image of God. Humanity was not made in the image of a power-hungry dictator. The dominion described is not one of conquering and crushing, but of multiplying and caring. We were not made in the image of an abstract thinker, or a passionless decision maker, or even a praise-hungry egotist. There is nothing in the text to suggest such notions.

The language used is the language of generosity to all, of relationality, of genuine unity amidst delightful diversity. Now, with man and woman in place, it was very good. In fact, Genesis 2 reiterates the creation account, underlining the same emphases. God provided abundantly and lavishly. Rivers, trees, fruit, life. And the greatest gift from Adam's perspective? When God introduced him to Eve, well, like many men since, the manual labourer became a poet!

The climax of the creation account is the ecstatic delight of Adam as he meets his bride. Thus, the creation account ends with a highlighter pen and double underlining to point us to the marital intent in everything: a man shall leave parents and be united to his wife, so that they, though two, shall be united as one. The Bible's great picture. God's great goal.

God wants the Bible reader to see, more than anything else, the great picture of marriage. This is not a result of the Fall into sin, or a pragmatic approach to societal structuring, or a contracted agreement for mutual stability and benefits. Marriage is the great picture of God's intent to unite the diverse into the delight of true unity. And what is hinted at here in Genesis 1-2 will blow our hearts and minds by the time we reach Revelation and the marriage described there at the climax of history. But the wonder of that great marriage will not be truly felt unless we first descend into the valley of the shadow of Genesis 3.

THE GREAT TWIST

The third chapter of Genesis should shock the unsuspecting first-time reader. At the same time it should ring true to all of us who live in this broken world. Everywhere we look we see the aftershocks of Genesis 3—in creation, on the news, in society, in the mirror. In fact, we tend not to see the effects enough. We fail to notice how everything we do, the plans we make, the motivations we justify, even the religious and charitable philanthropy we generate, are so saturated in a post-Genesis 3 brine that corruption runs to the core of everything.

The news is bad. Very bad. In fact, much worse than we have dared to imagine.

Eve got into a conversation with the serpent. He was crafty, inviting her to consider possibilities that had never before entered her consciousness. Can God be trusted? Is He really good? Does He want the best for you? Doesn't He really want you to be making up your own mind? Independence, self-determination, God-like autonomy ...

The invitation to doubt God's word and add the knowledge of evil to their experience of good, to taste and see that God is not all good and that death is a false threat, and that being like God is the way to go ... and within a few verses the fatal disease is contracted. It was not just the taking of the fruit. That was bad, of course. But it was the wanting to. She wanted to. Deceived, of course, but wanting to. And Adam too, standing there, not deceived, but his heart drove him to want the same.

They wanted, they took, they bit, they died. Or did they? Perhaps they just began to die. Perhaps God was not quite right when he said that 'in the day you eat of it you shall surely die' (Gen. 2:17). Maybe their bodies began to die, and maybe creation began to die, maybe the process of death entered through one man, but meanwhile they could strive to keep on living?

Here is the confusion in which we still live today. None of us believe we are really dead. Thousands of years later, a top religious leader came to Jesus for a conversation. Jesus basically refused. 'Nicodemus, we cannot talk about God stuff because you are a dead man, you need to be born from above before we can talk about God stuff!' (see John 3:1-15). Nicodemus, the teacher of Israel, of all people, the expert in Genesis 3 no less, even he didn't believe that he was dead! Neither do we.

Back to Genesis 3. If life consists in activity – independent breathing, independent decision-making, independent activity, etc. – then we are not actually dead. We may be dying, but we are not dead. But what if we are like goldfish that cannot see the water in which we continuously swim? What if we cannot see that the notion of independence *is* the very essence of death?

The clues in Genesis 1-2 are overwhelming. Life consists in divine generosity, mutual trust and relational unity in the midst of diversity. Life is not about independence and achievement, it is about connection and relationship.

Deep down, we all recognise that to be true. The greatest achievements in life – winning the tournament, receiving the doctorate, achieving promotion, earning a fortune ... they are all empty if we have no one to share them with. In fact, for many the greatest achievements are often followed by excessive drink or other experience-numbing escape routes. Why? Because all too often the achievement is hollow since marriage and family and friendship were compromised to achieve it. If life is about achievement and independence, then we may pour our energies into the pursuit, but the arrival tends to put the lie to it all.

Adam and Eve were alive in their relationship with God and each other, but they wanted independent God-like status. The God-likeness they wanted was a first-class lie. The only independent self-absorbed powerbroker deity figure is the fake god who was speaking with a hiss that day – the 'god' of this age. Yet still today we seem to believe that to be like God is to be independent and powerful and self-concerned and ... we are still dead in the lie that came with a hiss.

When they ate that fruit, they died.

Death was first and foremost in the soul. Their soul curved inwards. As Martin Luther put it, man is curved in on himself, and that is our problem. In fact, that is our death. Disconnected from God, we are dead. The bond that unites Father and Son in the triune God was withdrawn from the pinnacle of creation—the pair fashioned for fellowship with the Trinity. Now the Spirit that united them to each other and to God was gone. They wanted independence. God pulled back and let them have it.

The evidence of physical death took a while to manifest, but the evidence of spiritual/relational death was

25

immediate. They noticed for the first time that they were naked; they had never looked in that direction before. They began to cover themselves for the first time; they had never felt shame before. They hid from God; they had never felt the inclination towards separation before. They started to blame each other; they had never despised each other before. Welcome to death.

THE GREAT PROBLEM

Unless we really hear the Bible and grasp how deep the problem lies, we will always offer superficial explanations for sin: *Sin is trying hard, but not quite being good enough. Sin is about doing wrong. Sin is falling short so that if the pass mark is 50 out of 50, then our 49 is still not enough.*

Hang on. Where did talk of 49 out of 50 come from? The reality is that we are all at exactly 0 out of 50. Every single one of us is born dead in our sins. We are corrupt to the core. Some show that corruption in traditional sinful ways—the wild fist-shaking extravagance of rebellion in the far country. We all know what sin looks like: lust, theft, brutality, adultery, murder, deceit. But we fail to grasp that some show their absolute corruption in the other traditional sin mode—the self-righteous obedience of the religious son who stays at home.

When Jesus told the story of the two lost sons he set it up with two other stories (see Luke 15). A sheep lost in the far country, and a coin lost in the home. Then come the sons. The first rebels and heads off to Vegas or Amsterdam. He returns with his tail between his legs, his money spent, and his application speech lined up to become an employee who can earn benefits from a benevolent boss. The second stays home and works hard. The good son? Hardly. He also shames the father, views him as a boss, and demonstrates his incurved motivations. The father humiliates himself for both sons, longing for both to come in and enjoy more than his benefits, longing for fellowship and relationship.

Whether we are rebellious or religious, we are dead in sin. The only hope is something, or someone, who can draw us out of our obsessive self-love and back into life-giving fellowship with God.

In Genesis 3 they made false modesty masks. We still do the same. They made excuses. Us too. But God took charge of the situation. God knew that to clothe an immoral soul in an immortal body would be cruel in the extreme, so He barred access to the tree of life. Before that, He demonstrated that sin means death as He slaughtered animals and made a bloody cover for the guilty pair. And before that He made a promise.

Genesis 3:15. The gospel, 'take one': 'I will put enmity between you and the woman, between your seed and her seed. He shall crush your head, and you shall bruise his heel.' (Throughout the book I will use the term 'seed' in place of the typical 'offspring'. This helps to make the singular seed who fulfils God's plan more obvious to us.)

There is a solution to the devastation of sin and death. And it is not a 'what?' What shall we do? What can we say? What is required of us? None of that. The solution is a 'who?' He. The seed of the woman. As you read the Bible, be sure to be looking for him!

'I will make of you a great nation, and I will bless you and make your name great, so that you will be a blessing. I will bless those who bless you, and him who dishonours you I will curse, and in you all the families of the earth shall be blessed.' ... Then the LORD[1] appeared to Abram and said, 'To your offspring (seed) I will give this land.' So he built there an altar to the LORD, who had appeared to him.
- Genesis 12: 2-3, 7 -

That only-begotten Son, who today is for us 'the splendour of the glory of God the Father and the very stamp of his nature' (Heb. 1:3), became known of old to the Jews.[2]
- John Calvin -

---

1. When the Old Testament refers to God as LORD, all capitals, it is indicating that the name of God is in the underlying Hebrew. This four letter name, YHWH, was never spoken, but instead pronounced as the word 'Lord,' which then became the convention in translations, using all capitals to distinguish the name of God from the title of 'Lord.'

2. John Calvin, *Institutes of the Christian Religion*, 2.9.1, McNeil ed. (London: Westminster, 1960), p. 424.

2

The Presence of the Promiser

Genesis 12:1-3, 7

The problem of sin was launched by distrusting God's word. It will be solved by trusting God's word. All the way through the Bible we will find an emphasis on trusting what God has said. In fact, every narrative will bring us face to face with characters standing at a fork in the road. The constant choice before them, and before us, is this: will we trust God's word, or trust ourselves? The Bible gives us an epic showcase of what both choices will look like.

Consequently, since the notion of God's word is so critical, we must be sure to notice what God promises. We saw the great first glimpse of the gospel in Genesis 3:15. The solution to the sin problem is not a *what?* – i.e. what we must do – it is a *who*? The solution will be a 'he', the seed of the woman. And as we start looking for that seed, we will see the language of seed coming back at key moments in the text; special moments of divine promise.

There is an amazing pattern established back in Genesis 3. When humanity fails and we would expect God to wipe His hands of us and start again, God does the opposite. We fail, He adds detail to the promise. So failure in Genesis 3 is followed by promise in Genesis 3. How do things go after that? Not so well.

By chapter six we find God despairing at the sin of humanity. He has to wipe the planet to deal with the profound corruption. Sin followed by destruction, there, just as we'd expect. But then after graciously delivering Noah and his family, God makes a promise with Noah's seed (Gen. 9:9) and then points to Shem as the favoured line in whose tents God Himself would one day dwell (subtle, but see Gen. 9:27). So then all goes well? Not exactly. By chapter eleven we see the great sin of Babel – the gathering for anti-God achievement that has saturated human society ever since. So does God give up and start again? No, instead He gives His great promise to a pagan named Abram.

THE PROMISE TO ABRAM: THE SPINE OF THE BIBLE
The promise to Abram is the spine of the Bible. If we miss this, we'll struggle to make sense of everything from this point on. This descendent of Shem is the one who will be in the line of the coming seed. God promised to make him into a great nation. Where men had been trying to make a name for themselves, God promises to make Abram's name great. God promises to bless him, and to bless all the families of the earth in him.

What is this 'in him' idea? It becomes clear in 12:7 - God promises to give the special land to this man's seed. There it is, the seed! The promise of Genesis 12:2-3 is monumental, but don't miss the added P.S. in verse 7. That extra verse is massively significant. Perhaps more significant than we tend to notice (more of that later in the chapter).

The great promises of God to Abram take a while for him to grasp. He takes a while to fully leave his family. Eventually he separates from Lot and God immediately reiterates the seed promise (see Gen. 13:11-17). A bit more faith peeks through as Abram refuses the king of Sodom's offer of reward at the end of Genesis 14, and immediately God reiterates the seed promise in chapter 15. This time Abram believes the LORD, and it is counted to him as righteousness. Now the promise is ratified in a most formal covenant, and it is critical to see how Abram is passive in this great moment. God binds Himself to Himself to fulfil His word to Abram.

The Abram story is not about a promise given and believed, job done. It took years. It was quite a process. It contains strange failures and faithless moments. It contains the frailty of humans like Abram, like us. This grand narrative at the beginning of salvation history draws us in and comforts us. We may not believe immediately, we may fail and struggle, we may let God down, but God is loving and patient and diligent and determined. All the way through, God reiterated and restated the great promise.

THE PROMISE TO ABRAM DEVELOPED

The promise to Abram is developed in further promises as we read on through the Old Testament. Not only is it restated twice to Isaac and then Jacob, but also beyond the time of the Patriarchs, as God continues to develop His great promise-plan. We read how the nation is delivered from Egypt and they prove to be faithless in the wilderness. Does God give up? No. He adds to the promise. The promise of the land is developed in God's covenant with the nation at the end of Deuteronomy.

After the nation is in the land and the people prove to be utterly faithless, bottoming out in the four centuries of disaster covered by the book of Judges, does God give up on them? No. He adds to the promise. Specifically, His promise that the seed (plural) would become a nation with kings, this is developed in God's covenant with David in 2 Samuel 7.

After the nation is blessed during the golden years of David and Solomon, the nation divides and slides toward the disaster of invasion and the discipline of exile. Does God give up on them? No. He adds to the promise. God's promise of blessing is developed in the New Covenant that we will see in places like Jeremiah 31.

And after the exile the nation returns to the land with a whimper and seems to fall into the bleak emptiness of another four bad centuries, this time without even the book of Judges to offer hope. So does God give up on them? No. He fulfils the promise by sending the promised Seed. All of it comes together in the promise of the Seed singular, who we will fully meet in the New Testament!

So the history of humanity in a fallen world is the story of a God who promises and people who are fairly consistent in their failure to believe.

The critical issue is always whether people will respond to the generous loving-kindness and loyal faithfulness of God by trusting in His words of promise. Or whether they will despise Him and trust in themselves. As Paul shows later in Galatians 3:8 and Romans 4:10-12, this gospel was the good news of God's gift, not something God expected them to earn by their efforts. Indeed, Paul even zeroes in on the collective singular term 'seed' and underlines its importance to the whole gospel! Jesus would also tell the Jews that Abraham rejoiced to see His day (John 8:56). Somehow Abraham learned something of the divine provision for sin in the person of the coming Seed (see Genesis 22:5, 13-14 for a possible moment of clarity on such things!).

So as we trace through the highlights of the Old Testament we will see this promised Seed more clearly. We will feel our hearts stirred with anticipation to meet the *who?* of salvation.

THE PROMISE MAKER

As well as seeing the critical importance of God's great promise-plan we must not make a mistake that is sadly all too common. It seems that a growing number of people are putting emphasis on trusting in God's *promise*, but failing to notice the *God* who makes that promise.

Who it is that makes a promise is vitally important to whether or not we will trust that promise. If my neighbour kindly offers to look after my house and start my car while I am away on holiday, will I accept the offer and trust his promise to make sure all is safe and well? The promise is good, but I must consider who he is. If he has numerous driving convictions and was recently released from prison after spending his second spell inside for multiple counts of fraud and theft, perhaps I had better think twice before handing over my keys and heading to Spain!

If we read the Old Testament and only see behaviour requirements we are missing the point. But if we read the Old Testament and only see promises that must be trusted, we can still fall short of God's intent. If believing God's promises become a work that we do, then we have lost the heart of the Old Testament. God never intended Abraham or David to do the work of believing in unseen promises. He always invited them to trust not only His word, but to trust Him, the Promiser.

Can God be trusted? If the answer to the sin problem is not a what-must-we-do, but a who-can-we-trust, then we need to read our Bibles with eyes and hearts open to see the God who invites our trust. When we do that, what do we find?

THE PRESENCE OF THE PROMISER

We discover a God who constantly moves toward His creation to dwell in their midst. This is no distant God launching abstract truth missiles in our direction. This is a God who chooses to walk on two legs and dwell in the midst of His people.

Back in Genesis 3, who were Adam and Eve hiding from, then speaking to? It was God, walking in the garden to meet and talk with them. And since the Bible is clear that nobody has ever seen God the Father, then the LORD that they saw must be the LORD they were invited to look for. One day the Christophany (an appearance of Christ) would truly become flesh and dwell among them!

When the LORD added His P.S. to the promise of Genesis 12, in verse 7 we are twice told that the LORD appeared to Abram. The promise of the seed was made by God in person! The interaction that led up to Abram believing God and getting quoted in Romans was not mere trust in words, but it was trust in the Person who led him outside to show him the stars! The LORD appeared to him again in chapter 17:1; and again in 18:1, and in 18:22 we see that conversation continuing. In fact, the LORD appears at least seven times in Genesis.

In Genesis 26:2 He appears to Isaac and reiterates the great seed promise. He does the same in 26:24. As the promised line moves on, again to the unlikely son, Jacob, God steps in. This time Jacob is running scared of his elder brother Esau. Jacob was fearful and uncertain of the promise, but then God Himself steps in and wrestles with Jacob through the night. Jacob wrestles with God, sees His face, and lives! He is a changed man. Perhaps Jacob's real issue was not Esau, or Laban, or even himself; perhaps his real issue was that he didn't trust the Lord. After surviving that night, Jacob limps on ahead of his family with a newfound confidence in the Lord (see Gen. 32:30; 35:1; 35:10; cf. Hosea 12:2-5). Years later he would look back to meeting with God (Gen. 48:3).

As we read through the Old Testament we will see the promises pointing toward the coming seed. But we must not miss that God invited His people to trust in His *word,* that is, *His* word! They were invited not to the work of trusting, but to the privilege of trusting in response to a personal God. That invitation remains the same today.

As we go on through the Old Testament we will see the picture of the promised seed developing before our eyes. And at the same time we will see the presence of the One who promises, the One who invites us to trust in His word – that is, to trust in Him.

*'The Lord your God will raise up for you a prophet
like me from among you, from your brothers—it is
to him you shall listen ... I will raise up for them
a prophet like you from among their brothers. And
I will put my words in his mouth, and he shall speak
to them all that I command him.'*

- Deuteronomy 18:15, 18 -

*For at the end of the ages the Son himself spoke to us
through himself. No longer through the mediation of
a prophet or the voice of saints but through himself, the
only begotten, by being born into our condition, spoke with
us. And we say that the Father spoke in the Son, not as
through a human being somehow established as a special
kind of mediator or as one declaring a message to us which
was not his own but another's. Rather, the Son spoke to us
in his own voice through his own body. For the flesh be-
longed to the only begotten and not to anyone else. Though
God by nature, he became human while remaining God.*[1]

- Cyril of Alexandria -

*Therefore, in order that faith may find a firm basis for sal-
vation in Christ, and thus rest in him, this principle must
be laid down: the office enjoined upon Christ by the Father
consists of three parts. For he was given to be prophet, king,
and priest. Yet it would be of little value to know these
names without understanding their purpose and use.*[2]

- John Calvin -

---

1. Cyril of Alexandria, Commentary on Hebrews, in Pusey P.E., *Cyril of Alexandria* Volume 3 (Oxford, 1868-77), p. 364.

2. John Calvin, *Institutes of the Christian Religion*, 2.15.1, McNeil ed. (London: Westminster, 1960), p. 494.

3

The Prophet

Deuteronomy 18

The Old Testament promise of the coming seed-deliverer is not a set of random and obscure promises. It is a thread that works its way down through the generations. It continually points to God's faithfulness, not to human striving. It asks for trust, not effort; faith, not work. And along the way it is often surprising.

For instance, who would have expected God to resolve the sin problem caused by the woman's distrust through the male seed of a woman – how will a human put this right? Who would have expected God to plot the path of that promise through the seed of an elderly pagan from Ur in the Chaldees? Who would expect the promise to come through a son born of his aged wife, rather than the elder son born of the slave woman? Who would expect the second-born son of Isaac to be the one in line? Or who would expect Jacob's fourth son, rather than one of the first three, to continue that line of promise (Gen. 49:8-12)? And then after four centuries enslaved in Egypt, who would expect God to work through a stuttering old prince-turned-shepherd like Moses?

MOSES THE PROPHET

Moses was not in the line of the promised seed, but he got to hear about that promise. In fact, he heard about it from God. That is the amazing thing about Moses. Not just that he heard the promise reiterated, but that he met with God and so could represent God to the people. A man who can speak God's words to the people: weak Moses became a mighty prophet!

It all got launched when he met the angel of the LORD in Exodus 3. The burning-but-not-consumed bush got his attention, but the burning bush was just the stage. Within a few verses he could not look, for he was afraid to look at God. Months later he would look at God again.

Moses heard God speak of the seed promise at a key moment in his career. He had already led the nation out of Egypt as God delivered them with His mighty arm. He had led them through the Red Sea and on to Sinai. He had received the Ten Commandments. But all was not well. The faith of the people was shaky, to say the least. They didn't respond well to their deliverance, or to Sinai, or to the wilderness. And now, in chapter 32, Moses was taking a bit too long in his mountain-top meeting with the LORD.

So Aaron led the nation into wild spiritual adultery. He took their gold and forged a god in the image of the lie of Genesis 3 – that is, a god who is powerful, impressive, independent, self-absorbed. And the people acted like the 'god' they worshipped in wild self-gratification. And God, the jilted spouse, was fuming. In Exodus 32:10 the LORD is ready to consume the nation and turn His creative love toward Moses. So Moses quoted the great promise doctrine to God, and God relented from destroying the nation.

Moses came down to the people and expressed the heart of God in his zealous anger. The next day, Moses returned to the mountain-top for a meeting with the LORD. It was then, with God still angry, that Moses heard the seed promise in God's voice (Exod. 33:1-3). But now there was a change. God would fulfil His promise concerning the land, but He Himself would not go with them. Moses and the people were stunned.

Moses knew that blessing without the blesser was not enough, so he interceded again. God finally agreed to go with them. Then, out of the blue, Moses comes out with an awesome request 'Show me your glory!' (33:18).

MOSES REPRESENTED THE GOD HE MET!

Are you serious? Surely standing atop a mountain with the angry jilted spouse that is the LORD, the one whose presence could so easily consume His people, the one who had sent a plague on the people just verses earlier, surely Moses should be asking for the exit route, not the glory display!

What happens next becomes a critical moment in the history of God's people. The next few verses are referred to and alluded to within the Old Testament more than almost any other Old Testament text. God tells Moses that he cannot see His face, for nobody can see the face of the

LORD and live. Yet Moses will get to see the tail-end of God's passing glory. Face? No. Glory? Yes. Actually, it turns out that the LORD's face will make sense of the surprising request to see His glory.

The people had been scared of God's powerful glorious presence. They had pulled back from Sinai. Surely now Moses was in for it. Surely now he would be consumed in a glorious and bright power-display as God flexed His muscles before this elderly man? That is not what happened. Even with the text as clear as it is, people still portray God's glory display as nothing more than bright shiny power. But that is not what God says, and it is not what God shows.

God actually tells Moses, 'I will make all my goodness pass before you and will proclaim before you my name, "The LORD." And I will be gracious to whom I will be gracious, and will show mercy on whom I will show mercy' (Exod. 33:19). Hang on ... really? Goodness? Name? Gracious? Mercy? Is that God's glory?

Why are we surprised? Could it be that we are swimming in post-Genesis 3 waters and don't see how our conception of God has been perverted into a self-concerned, power-broker perversion of the real thing? Of course God is not to be taken lightly or treated faithlessly, and he underlines that in 34:6-7 when the glory encounter occurs. But the overwhelming majority of the content points to God's goodness, graciousness, mercy, slowness to anger, abounding in loving-kindness and faithfulness (in New Testament terms, that would be 'grace and truth'), forgiving iniquity, etc.

Why are we surprised? Does not the whole Bible reiterate God's loving-kindness and covenant loyalty again and again? Was not the creation account brimming over with God's glorious generosity and kindness? Was His faithful loyalty not proven again and again by the unfaithfulness of His people through each phase of biblical history? Perhaps we are surprised by God's response to Moses, not because we do not read our Bibles, but because if we do, we struggle to see what is there? Our vision is clouded by the Genesis 3 twisting of what God is really like.

THE FACE AND THE GLORY

So how does the LORD's face help us with the request to see His glory here? The reason Moses had the confidence to ask the LORD to see His glory at the end of Exodus 33 is because he already knew the LORD face to face, as described earlier in the same chapter. Moses, we are told, would head out to the tent of meeting down on the level of the people, and there he would meet the LORD face to face, as a man speaks with his friend (see verses 7-11).

Now that is confusing. In verse 11 he speaks with the LORD face to face. By verse 20 the LORD tells him that he cannot see His face and live. Schizophrenic God? Clumsy editing by the compiler of the text? Or perhaps another explanation is in order. Perhaps the LORD up high on the mountain cannot be seen by humans, but the LORD whose tent is pitched down nearer the camp can be seen face to face? Perhaps Moses had confidence in requesting a glory display from the LORD on the mountain because he had grown to know the character of the LORD in his meetings in the tent? How can there be two LORDs, but one LORD? That is a question worth hanging on to as we read on in the Old Testament.

Moses encountered the LORD face to face, and so Moses was a great prophet. He met Him at the burning bush in Exodus 3, and then went to Pharoah and represented God to the most powerful man on earth. He regularly met the LORD in the tent of meeting, and led the nation through the wilderness as God's spokesman. Back in Exodus 24 Moses was not alone when he saw God, but after that it tended to be just him (with Joshua his assistant nearby). God Himself underlined the unique access Moses had in Numbers 12:6-8 (see also Num. 14:14).

Moses and the Seed Promise

Fast-forward to the next generation and a now very elderly Moses is still leading the people. A generation had to be wiped out for their faithlessness, but now the new generation were preparing to enter the land God had promised. At such a momentous point in their history we would expect to see references to the seed promise again, and we do.

Moses launches Deuteronomy with a quote from God, urging the nation to go in and take possession of the land that the LORD swore to their fathers, to Abraham, to Isaac, and to Jacob, to give to them and to their seed forever (Deut. 1:8)! He finishes this first section with another reference to the seed, this time underlining that it was God's love for their fathers that led to the choosing of the seed and the nation's deliverance by God's own presence (4:37).

Again Moses points to the love of God as the driving force in choosing the seed (corporate), as represented in the nation that were now called to circumcise their hearts in faithful response to this loving God (Deut. 10:15-16). In the wrapping up of the great land covenant we find the same language of circumcised hearts in the seed (corporate) being used to urge the nation to love God and live (Deut. 30:6).

One last time Moses hears reference to the seed promise. He is standing on Mount Nebo surveying the land. The LORD restates His great promise to Abraham, Isaac and Jacob, to give the land to their seed. But Moses will not go in. His journey is over. The great leader and prophet, God's spokesman, dies (Deut. 34:6).

Would there ever be another prophet like Moses? A man who knew the LORD face to face and could represent Him to the people? The last verses of Deuteronomy (34:10-12) suggest not. At least, not at the time those verses were written!

THE PROPHET LIKE MOSES

However, back in Deuteronomy 18 we have another critical prediction in the line of the promised seed. From verses 15 to 22, Moses tells the nation that one day God will raise up a prophet like him. This coming prophet will be Jewish, and he will be fully authorised to declare God's word with absolute authority. For a prophet to be truly like Moses he would need to perform wonders, be able to give God's Law, pray for his people and deliver them too.

It is no surprise that the Jews in Jesus' day expected the Messiah to be 'the Prophet' like Moses. When Jesus performed wonders, they asked if this could be the Prophet (see John 6:14). Even the Samaritan woman anticipated the coming of this Prophet (John 4:19, 29). When Peter preached in Acts 3:11-26, he was clear that Jesus was indeed that Prophet, and Stephen made the same connection in Acts 7:37.

So the seed promise continues to wend its way through the canon. And the promised seed becomes ever clearer in definition. He would be a prophet, like Moses. But there is more.

And I will raise up for myself a faithful priest, who shall do according to what is in my heart and in my mind. And I will build him a sure house, and he shall go in and out before my anointed for ever.
- 1 Samuel 2:35 -

The eternal Son of God did clothe himself with the infirmities of our flesh, and left the company of those innocent and blessed spirits, who knew well how to love and adore him, that he might dwell among men, and wrestle with the obstinacy of that rebellious race, to reduce them to their allegiance and fidelity, and then to offer himself up as a sacrifice and propitiation for them.

I remember one of the poets hath an ingenious fancy to express the passion wherewith he found himself overcome after a long resistance: 'That the god of love had shot all his golden arrows at him, but could never pierce his heart, till at length he put himself into the bow, and darted himself straight into his breast.' Methinks this doth some way adumbrate God's method of dealing with men: he had long contended with a stubborn world, and thrown down many a blessing upon them; and when all his other gifts could not prevail, he at last made a gift of himself, to testify his affection and engage theirs.[1]
- Henry Scougal, *The Life of God in the Soul of Man* -

---

1.   Henry Scougal, *The Life of God in the Soul of Man* (Boston, 1868), p. 110-11.

4

The Priest

1 Samuel 2

Once we leave the books of Moses we carry with us the dual threads of the seed promise and the presence of the Promiser. Both remain critical, but not consistently central. Things start well with Joshua. His years of learning at Moses' side have set him up well to be the new leader of the nation.

The book launches with God speaking to Joshua and assuring him of God's intent to fulfil, in Joshua, His promises to Moses, as well as continuing to be with him as He had been with Moses. Promise. Presence. Perfect.

GOD WALKING ON TWO LEGS
Turn the page and Israel is preparing for the first great battle in the land, 'unconquerable' fortress Jericho. At the end of

chapter 5, Joshua looks up and sees a man. This man turns out to be the commander of the armies of the LORD. Is this a high-ranking angel? No, He's higher than that. Joshua falls to the ground in worship, and is told what Moses had been told at the burning bush. Holy ground: sandals off!

The doctrine of the presence of God dwelling amidst His people is a thrilling chase through the canon. There was the Garden of Eden. Then Abraham, Isaac, Jacob and Moses. There was the special presence of God in the pillar of fire and cloud in the wilderness. Now Joshua meets Him. God does not ask His people to trust in an abstract promise, but in the promise of His own Person.

But after Joshua, things go downhill. The book of Judges has to be one of the most depressing accounts in the Bible. Four centuries marked by the sinfulness of God's people. Sure, God delivers them when they cry out in desperation, but it never takes long for them to grow complacent and go back to doing what seems right in their own eyes (see Judg. 17:6 and 21:25). Even the people God uses as heroic deliverers often give the sense of simply being the best options available during corrupt times.

Yet in the midst of this discouraging book we still see God choosing to visit His people. The Angel of the LORD seems unusually active. Is this just an angel, or is this the messenger of God's presence? Well, the whole nation heard Him and wept in 2:1-4. Gideon was called during an appearance of this messenger (6:11-24), and the text becomes overt that it was the LORD meeting with Gideon, who in turn grows fearful, for he has seen His face!

Manoah's wife is visited by a 'man of God' who is the angel of the LORD (13:3, 6). Manoah prays to God asking for the man to return, God hears him and sends the angel again (13:8-22). During the ensuing interaction, Manoah discovers that the 'man of God' has a 'wonderful' name (cf. Isa. 9:6), and eventually discovers, to his dread, that they have seen God!

The presence of God walking with His people is a thrill to see, but what about the growing problem of sin? Anticipating a prophet who can represent God to the people is great, but what about someone who can represent the sinful people to God? What about a priest?

THE PEOPLE'S REPRESENTATIVE: A PRIEST

The last of the Judges is the greatest of them all. He comes after the book of Judges, and has books named after him: Samuel. His story begins with his barren mother, the godly Hannah. She comes before an ungodly high priest whose dysfunctional family demonstrates just how far the priesthood has collapsed.

The priesthood was established back in the times of Moses. While it was God's intent that Israel be a kingdom of priests, that role became more narrowly defined as their growing sin prompted greater specificity in the Law given to the nation. Their unfaithfulness in the Golden Calf incident led to what is sometimes known as the Priestly Code – a body of laws stretching right the way through Leviticus 16, the great chapter on the Day of Atonement. Sin was deadly serious and sinful people needed to be carefully represented before a holy God. (Incidentally, further illegitimate worship, this time by the people, in Leviticus 17 led to the last block of legal code, addressing further issues of purity amongst the people as a whole.)

By the time we come to Eli's day, the priesthood is broken beyond recognition. Indeed, the old man has one last role to play in introducing Hannah's miracle boy to the Lord, then his household is finished.

Hannah was a poor farmer's wife. She was barren and desperately wanted a child. The elderly priest couldn't spot piety when it knelt praying before him, but God heard her prayer. Once the boy was weaned, Hannah brought him back to the tabernacle. Her desire was profoundly godly: she wanted him to be in the presence of the LORD and dwell there forever (1 Sam. 1:22). Little did she know that this miracle boy would be the last of the judges, the first of a long line of prophets, and the transition figure between the period of the Judges and the monarchy. In fact, things had become so bad that by now we should be expecting God to step in and add some details to His great seed promise before too long!

In response to God's goodness Hannah prays a magnificent prayer, demonstrating that she had spent much time pondering the Scriptures. The central focus of her prayer? God and His anointed King! Where did that thought come from? Well, from the Scriptures, of course. Hannah would have known of God's promise of kings from Abraham (Gen. 17:6, 16), and the symbols of authority stated to Judah (Gen. 49:10) and also the coming king's conquering exploits as described by Balaam (Num. 24:17). Now Hannah adds more detail: he will judge the whole earth (1 Sam. 2:10)!

Her little boy would be the transition to monarchy in Israel, and the prelude to the great next stage in the seed promise as details of the coming King would blossom into detail.

But this coming king would need to judge precisely because of the great sin problem, which brings our thoughts back to the need for a priest.

THE PRIEST PREDICTED

Just as the promise of the king was developing, so was the notion of a coming priest. The priestly system seen in the books of Moses had collapsed almost beyond recognition by this point. In fact, the priest-like intercession of Moses himself seemed a distant memory by the time of Eli and his delinquent sons. But this is the moment for a greater priest to be predicted!

God had already established an 'everlasting' priesthood with Aaron's grandson Phinehas (Num. 25:12-13). Now, centuries later, we see God ending the line with Eli's sons being killed. What about the forever aspect of the priesthood? Actually, somewhere in the time of the Judges, the priestly line had switched from the line of Eleazer and Phinehas to Aaron's other son Ithamar. Eli was a descendent of Ithamar, and it was time for this mess to be fixed.

In 1 Samuel 2:27-36 an unnamed prophet comes to Eli and gives him a message from the LORD. Enough was enough. Eli had honoured his sons more than God, but they were a disaster. Indeed, they would both die on the same day as a sign to Eli (see ch. 4). But God would raise up a faithful high priest who would truly honour all that was on God's heart and mind (1 Sam. 2:35).

But then God adds that this priest shall have a lasting household, and 'he shall go in and out before my anointed forever.' So if the priest is serving before the Messiah, he cannot be the Messiah, right? Right. Unless it is the household of the priest that goes in and out before him, the Messiah-priest. Is that possible? The text certainly allows it, and in verse 30 the idea of a household going in and out before God is already established in the text.

In the next chapter young Samuel is called by God. Just a voice calling in the night? *The LORD came and stood, calling as at other times, 'Samuel! Samuel!'* (1 Sam. 3:10). The presence of the Promiser!

This is not a familiar text, but it does stand as a significant pointer as the picture of the coming Messiah develops. He will be a prophet like Moses. He will be a faithful priest, unlike Eli.

PRIEST AND SACRIFICE

This is not the only place we see the Messianic figure anticipated in priestly terms. Consider the great Royal Psalm – Psalm 110. One of the most quoted Psalms in the New Testament, this Psalm of David anticipates the coming King, but it also views Him as a priest. Not an ordinary priest, but one in the order of Melchizedek. This idea is picked up later in Hebrews 7.

One more piece we must notice before we move on: priests offer sacrifices to God for the sins of the people. This might be considered the great surprise of the New Testament, the coming anointed priest would offer the greatest sacrifice: Himself! But the clues are there for those with eyes to see.

Isaiah does not just anticipate the coming king, as we will see in the next chapter, but also the suffering servant of the LORD who is Himself the great substitutionary sacrifice in the fourth servant song (Isa. 52:13-53:12).

In the Psalms we catch glimpses of the anointed greater son of David being rejected (Ps. 118), betrayed (Ps. 69), and dying (Ps. 22 and 16).

The great sin problem of Genesis 3 was never resolved by the priestly system made up of sinful men. But the solution would ultimately be a priestly One. Only, this Priest would be altogether different. He had to be the promised anointed One Himself, the faithful Priest who alone could make the necessary sacrifice to atone for the sin of humanity.

The Prophet, the Priest, and then, of course, the coming King...

When your days are fulfilled and you lie down with your fathers, I will raise up your offspring (seed) after you, who shall come from your body, and I will establish his kingdom.
- 2 Samuel 7:12 -

*For to us a child is born,
to us a son is given;
and the government shall be upon his shoulder,
and his name shall be called
Wonderful Counselor, Mighty God,
Everlasting Father, Prince of Peace.
Of the increase of his government and of peace
there will be no end,
on the throne of David and over his kingdom,
to establish it and to uphold it
with justice and with righteousness
from this time forth and forevermore.
The zeal of the LORD of hosts will do this.*
– Isaiah 9:6-7 –

God is our King before the worlds. Since God always reigns and is omnipotent, with what view do those who call God 'Father' offer up to him their requests and say, 'Your kingdom come'? They seem to desire to behold Christ the Saviour of all rising again upon the world. He will come.[1]
- Cyril of Alexandria -

---

1.   Cyril of Alexandria, *Commentary on Luke, Homily 73*.

5

The King

---

2 Samuel 7; Isaiah 9; Micah 5

For centuries the great seed promise of God had been past action. That is, God had referred to it in hindsight to Isaac, Jacob, Moses and so on. During the wilderness years, the unusual character Balaam had anticipated a future king descended from Jacob (see Num. 24:17), but not since the days of Abraham had the seed promise really been driven forward. That is, until David.

KING DAVID
The nation transitioned from the period of the Judges to a monarchy under the sometimes despairing watch of Samuel. God had given the nation a king – the kind they desired. Saul was a disaster. Then Samuel was sent on a mission to

Bethlehem to pick God's choice, the king whose household was anticipated in the days of Abraham, Judah, Balaam and Hannah. As ever, the choice was not obvious.

It is God's pattern to overlook the eldest, the biggest and the strongest. Sorry Ishmael, Esau, Reuben, Simeon, Levi. This time the choice was not the second-born, nor the fourth, but the eighth. Take a bow, young David! While people look for independent power figures like Saul (seeing through the clouded lens of a post-Genesis 3 world), God looks intently at the heart. David was a man with a heart pointed in God's direction (see 1 Sam. 13:14; 16:7).

The story of David's rise to power is long and complex. Eventually he became the king he had long been anointed to become. He conquered Jerusalem and made it his capital. He brought the Ark of the Covenant back to Jerusalem. Then in 2 Samuel 7 comes the high point of his career!

David looked out of his royal palace and saw God's Ark dwelling in a very old tent. He noted this anomaly to Nathan who urged him to do whatever he felt best. But that night God stopped Nathan in his tracks and sent him back to David with a great promise. David would not build God a house, but God would build David a household – a forever dynasty, a lasting throne, and a seed to sit on that throne forever (see 2 Sam. 7:12-16).

David was blown away. He could tell this promise was bigger than just the promise of a son. Somehow this seemed to point to a greater Son. While some details fit his son Solomon, some certainly didn't. David went in and sat before the Lord (David's many Psalms underline for us that David was a man who knew the Promiser, and not just the promise!). Now he exclaimed that God's goodness to him was too overwhelming to describe. After all that God had done, now He promised something stretching off into the distant future, and His throne would be the source of instruction for humanity as a whole (2 Sam. 7:19). What a kingdom that would be! Surely God would one day bring blessing to all the families of the earth (Gen. 12:3).

After the gospel given in Genesis 3:15 and then the great promise to Abraham in Genesis 12, this is the next great instalment in the line of the promised seed. Intriguingly, David refers to God as 'Adonai Yahweh' (translated typically as Lord GOD) five times during his great prayer (2 Sam.7:18-29). This is intriguing because the last time that title was used for God was in Genesis 15:8, when the LORD ratified the covenant with Abraham! David certainly seems to grasp the significance of the 'seed' promise being given here.

From this point on, the whole of the Old Testament looks back to God's promise to David in 2 Samuel 7 (This is also found in 1 Chron. 17, as well as the extended commentary given in Ps. 89).

Is this Him?

Once God had promised the coming of the seed of the woman, Eve naturally looked for him. She thought Cain was the one, then perhaps Seth. Now the great promise to David prompted a continual awareness of the throne of David. Solomon followed, starting well, but eventually was led astray by a heart not fully gripped by God (even though at the outset of his career, he also got to see the presence of the Promiser! See 1 Kings 3:5). A privileged start, a drifting heart, and finally the nation divided! Disaster!

The United Kingdom of Israel had lasted only three kings, and from this point on the divided nation seemed to descend ever closer to divine discipline. In the Northern Kingdom there was continual transfer of dynasties, each one measured against the definitive godless rebel, King Ahab. But in the Southern Kingdom, with Jerusalem as the capital, the Davidic dynasty passed on from generation to generation. With each new king, perhaps now the promise would be fulfilled?

Part of the great promise to David identified the coming seed of David as the son of God. This seemed to register with David as something more than just a title for a king (although it was used that way at times). For instance, in Psalm 2 (assuming that David wrote this Psalm – see Acts 4:25), we read of the LORD establishing His king on Zion, who is then referred to as the Son. This Son of Yahweh is massively significant. So much so that all the kings of the earth must be sure to honour and embrace this Son as the key to their own security and future.

In Psalm 110 David explicitly refers to his Lord as the King that is at the right hand of the LORD. This coming son of David is so great that David looks to him as his own Lord.

The coming greater son of David becomes a major theme throughout the divided monarchy and the ministry of the writing prophets. Let us grab a couple of highlights:

Micah – Sometimes dubbed the mini-Isaiah, it is easy to overlook Micah. We must not do so. He offers the reader some heart-stirring anticipation of the coming king, not to mention some clarification on location and identity.

He is famous for the location information in chapter 5, but before we go there, we must not miss the end of chapter 2. After two chapters of bleak critique of Jerusalem and Samaria (as representative capital cities of the divided kingdom), with anticipation of coming judgment, finally there is a burst of hope in 2:12-13. God promises to gather His people like sheep in a pen, another one of many iterations of the theme of God's regathering His people

Israel. But then in verse 13 we see the people will be led out by their king. Here's the Messiah, the King. And in typical Hebrew parallel form, His identity is clarified in the next line. It is the LORD at their head.

We are not in the Psalms, but *Selah* (a term typically understood to mean something like 'pause and ponder'). The Messianic King that will lead his people is actually the LORD? Perhaps the Promiser and the promise are two sides of the same thematic ribbon?

The next chunk of Micah offers much more than just two verses of hope; this time there are two whole chapters. Chapter 4 looks forward to a time when Zion will be the centre-point of God's work in the world, a place of both throne and teaching (as in the promise to David in 2 Sam. 7:19). And it goes on to anticipate the coming ruler, the Messianic King. He will come from the little town of David – Bethlehem. And He will be a ruler whose 'goings forth are from of old' – the word here is often used to refer to eternity. Again, Micah is pointing to the divine identity of the Messianic King.

Incidentally, before leaving Micah we must notice the final verses of the third great section of the book. In 7:18-20 Micah lives up to his name (who is like the LORD?) by asking that very question. Who is a God like this one, who forgives, pardons, loves steadfastly, shows compassion and faithfulness? It sounds like an Exodus 34 remix! And Micah ends with total trust in God's loyalty to the promises made to Abraham and the Patriarchs!

Isaiah – From the mini-Isaiah to the man himself. Surely Isaiah is the great book of the coming Messiah! This great book offers three great portraits of the Messiah: (1) the King, (2) the Servant of the LORD, and (3) the Anointed Conqueror.

Before we consider the presentation of the coming King, we must notice the presence of the King! In Isaiah 6 we read of the prophet's call. It was the year Uzziah died (740 B.C.). Many had had high hopes for Uzziah. Perhaps he would be the one? Now, after a very long reign, he was dead. Nothing like the death of a strong monarch to cause instability. But all was well. Isaiah got to see the heavenly throne, and on it, he saw the LORD! What a privilege. Again, the presence of God. Who did Isaiah see? John 12:40-41 tells us that Isaiah saw Jesus, the Lord. The presence of the Promiser, who stands behind, and is Himself the promise in whom they were invited to trust.

So what does Isaiah have to say about the coming King? In the section following his prophetic call Isaiah offers several critical insights into the Messianic King. The current man on David's throne was Ahaz, and he was facing the great Assyrian threat as well as more local political threats against the Davidic throne. God invites Ahaz to request a sign of the divine faithfulness to the ancient promise, but Ahaz declines (trusting self instead of trusting God). The sign is offered nonetheless. What follows is the great Immanuel sequence.

First comes the promise of a virgin giving birth to a child (7:14), and by the end of the sequence we have the announcement of the greatest birth – the new leader that would be born (9:6-7). It will be a male child, whose government will be forever, and whose titles build on each other to thrill the reader. Wonderful Counselor – whose wisdom will accomplish the greatest of challenges. Mighty God – again we discover that the Messianic ruler will be divine. Everlasting Father – the term typically used of the LORD reinforces the identity of this ruler. Prince of Peace

– His rule will bring all the blessings of peace. The ruler is destined to sit on David's throne.

And there's more. In chapter 11, Isaiah anticipates a future for the covenant programme beyond the current crises. The shoot from the stump of Jesse will be anointed by the Spirit of God in order to be an effective ruler and administrator. His rule will be truly just and peaceful; even nature itself will be transformed.

Daniel – The lengthy Aramaic section of Daniel 2-7 begins and ends with chapters concerned with a sequence of four successive world empires. In both chapters the empires are impressive, but the greatest impact follows as God's kingdom is established to fill the earth. In chapter 2 the image is a rock growing into a mountain. But in chapter 7:13 Daniel sees 'one like a son of man' coming on the clouds of heaven, standing beside the throne and given dominion. Again in 9:24-27 Daniel is pointed toward the coming ruler, this time described as an anointed prince, who would be cut off.

Zechariah – After the exile the prophets continued to anticipate the coming King. In Zechariah 6, for instance, we read of the coming Priest-King who will rebuild the temple and sit on the throne. In chapter 9:9-10 the prophet describes the coming of the King to Jerusalem, His righteous character, the disarmament of the world and His peaceful reign. The good shepherd is rejected in 11:4-14 and the Messiah is pierced in 12:10. Zechariah is not an easy book, but it is brimming over with the Messianic anticipation!

As you read through the Old Testament let the anticipation build, for the prophet, the priest, the king is coming!

*'For this is the covenant that I will make with the house of Israel after those days, declares the L*ORD*: I will put my law within them, and I will write it on their hearts. And I will be their God, and they shall be my people. And no longer shall each one teach his neighbour and each his brother, saying, "Know the L*ORD*," for they shall all know me, from the least of them to the greatest, declares the L*ORD*. For I will forgive their iniquity, and I will remember their sin no more.'*

- Jeremiah 31:33-34 -

When we read in sacred history what God did, from time to time, towards His Church and people, and how He revealed Himself to them, we are to understand it especially of the Second Person of the Trinity. When we read of God appearing after the fall, in some visible form, we are ordinarily, if not universally, to understand it of the Second Person of the Trinity… John 1:18. He is therefore called the image of the invisible God – Col 1:15 – intimating that though God the Father be invisible, yet Christ is His image or representation, by which He is seen.[1]

- Jonathan Edwards, *A History of the Work of Redemption* -

---

1.   Jonathan Edwards, *A History of the Work of Redemption* in *The Works of Jonathan Edwards*, Vol.9 (Yale, 1989).

6

The Covenant in Person

Jeremiah; Ezekiel; Isaiah

All was not well. By the time you get towards the end of the Old Testament it should be evident that humanity has a big problem. The hiss of Genesis 3 can be heard in the rebellion of humanity against God. And if we listen carefully, that hiss can be heard in the religiosity of humanity too.

Throughout the Old Testament we read of God's steadfast love and faithfulness. That is the diamond shown against the black velvet of human rebellion and sin. Even God's chosen people, Israel, with all their advantages, were still riddled with sin.

The lingering lie of Genesis 3 will always convince us that we can be like God, that we can be independent and do it all ourselves. Some will rebel and live godless lives. Others will commit to religious activity. But both are living the lie of God-like independence. The lie was not just to suggest that humans could attain to God's position, it was a lie about the nature of God Himself, for He is not committed to a self-serving independence.

So the Old Testament leaves us with a tension to resolve. Godless rebellion is to be condemned. Yet at the same time, supposedly godly religion is equally critiqued by God who seems to care about the heart attitudes of the people. So where does the solution lie? What, or who, can come and fix this mess?

THE PROFOUND PROBLEM

You do not want to receive care from a doctor too quick to prescribe before an accurate diagnosis. A cast on the arm does nothing for a sprained ankle. Right diagnosis must precede helpful prescription. So what is the diagnosis? What is the lingering problem of humanity in the Old Testament?

Too often we settle for a paper-thin diagnosis. Unsurprisingly, we then end up with a paper-thin solution.

The heart of the human problem is not misbehaviour. Our problem is not that we just are not quite good enough. We don't score 49 out of 50, and only just fall short of the glory of God. The reality is that all of us are at precisely 0 out of 50. Our problems are not merely behavioural, they spew forth from the root of all that we are and do: *The heart of the human problem is the human heart!*

And what is wrong with our hearts? We have bought into the lie. We want to be God. We don't want God to be God. At the core of who we are we are lovers of self and haters of God. Some will shake their fist at heaven, others will treat God as a benefactor and distributor of personal blessings, but either way: we don't love God.

As God-haters we are not only corrupted at the heart level, we are also dead towards God because we have nothing of His grace dwelling in us by His Spirit. God is alien to us. There is no connection.

We cannot force ourselves to love something we don't. So what in the world can change the human heart? Perhaps the better question is this: what from out of this world can come and change the human heart?

THE SUPREME SOLUTION: PART ONE – THE PROMISE

As we have seen already, human failure and rebellion lead to God adding detail to His most gracious plan. So the prophets point the reader to God's great promise of the New Covenant. If we are gripped by the disaster of human sin, heart-level death and hatred of God, then the prophets should shake us to the core!

Here is a hypothetical question to ponder. Imagine meeting a Jew. A real Hebrew-Bible-reading, synagogue-committed Jew. Ask them about the covenant God made with Israel in the days of Moses. Don't you think they could do a good job of explaining and even quoting that covenant? The blessings and the curses, even the Laws? And I don't just mean Ten Commandments, I suspect they could cite hundreds of the 613 laws.

Now imagine meeting a follower of Christ. You know, a church-attending, Bible-reading, believing Christian. Ask him or her about the New Covenant, the centrepiece of current connection between God and humanity. Could they give the details? Could they list the five or so main provisions of the New Covenant? What about the person in the mirror, how would you get on?

Isn't it strange that we are so convinced being a follower of Christ is worth staking our eternity on, yet most of us are unable to list just five main points of the New Covenant?

So what are these five main points of God's prescription for our greatest problem of guilt, absolute heart disease and total separation from God?

Jeremiah had a tough job. He spoke for God to a nation on the brink of exile. Their hard-heartedness towards God and their flagrant spiritual adultery meant that discipline was imminent. And yet Jeremiah gave them, and us, the ground-zero New Covenant passage.

Despite the total faithlessness of God's people, Jeremiah was able to speak of a future day when they would be His people and He would be their God (30:22). They had gone off after other lovers who all came to nought, but God was faithful and He was with them to save them (see 30:10-14).

In chapter 31 God begins by looking back to His loving them with an everlasting love, faithfully being with them, even appearing to them. In the future the faithless people of God will be satisfied with His goodness. So to ground-zero: Jeremiah 31:31.

There is a New Covenant coming, and it is different from what was given before. God had been a husband to them, but they had been unfaithful. In the future, God would put the law in their hearts, He would be their God (they'll all 'know the LORD') and their sins will be forgiven.

Here are three elements of the New Covenant:

1. Sins forgiven. After all they had done, and said, and thought. After all we have done, and said, and thought. Sins forgiven. What a thought. Not sins temporarily covered over, or sins hypothetically overlooked. Sins forgiven. Fully. Finally. Freely. Forever. Gone. In the words of the hymn:

> My sin, O the bliss, of this glorious thought,
> my sin not in part but the whole,

Is nailed to the cross and I bear it no more,
praise the Lord, praise the Lord, O my soul![2]

That is the bit we tend to dwell on. Most of church life seems to revolve around proclaiming and celebrating the forgiveness of sins. It certainly is and should be a central feature of our faith, don't get me wrong. But actually, it gets even better!

2. Law in the heart. Instead of striving to do what we don't actually want to do, this is speaking of actually wanting to live for God's pleasure from the heart. If our heart is the real issue in our sin, then God promising to do something to our hearts is really good news!

3. Relationship with God. Somehow the separation is overcome, and humanity can be brought back into the relationship that we were designed to enjoy: fellowship with God. Jeremiah looked forward to the day when people would not even need to introduce their neighbour to the LORD, because everyone would know Him. That day is still future, but for us, the privilege of being His people and having Him as our God, and knowing the LORD, that day is now!

Ezekiel builds the picture further. Slightly overlapping with Jeremiah, Ezekiel was a priest and prophet whose temple connections gave him a passion for the presence of God. He got to see the harrowing sight of God's Spirit departing from the temple in Jerusalem – three of the saddest chapters in the Bible (Ezek. 9-11). By the mid-point of chapter 11 the future looks totally bleak. The prophet cried out asking God if there could be any future for the people.

---

2.   Horatio Spafford, 'When Peace Like a River.' 1874.

There was a future. God would bring the nation back from where it would be scattered. Then God also promised a heart change, and the presence of a new spirit within them. The stony, dead, unresponsive heart would be replaced by a living, fleshy, beating heart! And that heart would mean that they would live for God, obeying Him, and again, they will be His people and He will be their God! The whoring nation with a sick heart would be given an everlasting covenant (see also chapter 16).

In chapter 34 God turns His attention to the shepherds leading the people. These men were both evil and useless, and the people were hopelessly lost without a shepherd. But God promised that one day He would be the shepherd coming to search for the sheep, rescuing them and carrying them home from the far country. Then God returns to the theme of the future covenant of peace. There would be blessings on the people in their land, provision and protection. As a result, they would know they are His people, and that He is their God.

By chapter 36, God the jealous husband is angry at the nations, but comforting to His own. The return of the people would not be just an exercise in logistics. He would cleanse them from their sins. And again He promises to give them both a new heart and a new Spirit. The heart would be a living one, and the Spirit would be God's! The combination of heart and Spirit would bring about the transformation of sinners into faithful followers. In fact, again, they will be His people and He will be their God!

After the famous dry bones illustration of the giving of the Spirit in chapter 37, he underlines the life-giving nature of this future Covenant. God speaks of uniting the nation, and twice more, of their being His people and His being their God! The great hope is that God will dwell in the midst of His people again (Check out the last verse in Ezekiel to reinforce that hope!).

So here is the New Covenant in five:

1. Sins forgiven.

2. Law in the heart.

3. Living heart – here is Ezekiel's added dimension, as stone gets replaced from without by a living, fleshy heart!

4. Relationship with God.

5. Indwelling Spirit of God – one more addition from Ezekiel, the future dwelling of God's Spirit with man, in the human heart!

But there is one more feature, and for that we need to visit **Isaiah**.

THE SUPREME SOLUTION: PART 2 – THE PERSON
The glorious future New Covenant is not just a deal between God and man. It is a person between God and man! In the second 'half' of Isaiah the prophet introduces us to the Servant of the LORD. The famous Servant Songs offer so much insight into the manner and mission of this suffering servant. Be sure to read them in 42:1-4; 49:1-6; 50:4-9; and 52:13-53:12 ... but also be sure to read what follows these songs.

The first song (42:1-4) focuses on what the Servant will achieve: He will bring justice to the nations. But He will not be some overbearing super-headteacher whipping the school of humanity into shape. He will not be self-promotional or domineering. He will care tenderly for the weak and feeble.

After the song comes comment from the LORD concerning his servant. Here we find a startling development in our understanding of the covenant theme: 'I will give you as a covenant for the people, a light for the nations…'(42:6). The Servant of the LORD Himself is the covenant. This is not just a new way of working, a new deal between God and His people. The covenant God plans to give is the Servant that He delights in!

The second song (49:1-6) describes the thorough preparation of the Servant, including the struggle that He goes through. The song culminates in a description of the global goal of the Servant: not only to bring back the nation of Israel, but to be a light for all the nations, this will be the Messiah for all peoples so 'that my salvation may reach to the end of the earth'(v. 6).

Following the song, we again read words from the LORD, and again the same covenant information is revealed. In verse 8 God says, 'I will keep you and give you as a covenant to the people.'

As we read on through Isaiah we find another covenant reference in the follow-up to the final Servant Song. In chapter 54 God calls for celebration because the Creator is married to His people and He will gather them with compassion and everlasting love and His covenant of peace will not be removed. In 59:21 (see also 61:1-8) God again describes His covenant with the people as the Spirit-anointed Redeemer, that is, the Messiah Himself.

Sins forgiven, living hearts, transformed motivation, the Spirit given, restored relationship with God – all because of the coming of the Messiah, Himself the covenant between God and humanity. The New Covenant is well worth anticipating. In fact, let's get past that blank page in our Bibles and meet Him in the flesh!

PART TWO:

Immanuel, God With Us
Matthew 1–2

The book of the genealogy of Jesus Christ,
the son of David, the son of Abraham.
- Matthew 1:1 -

A sign shall be given
A virgin will conceive
A human baby bearing
Undiminished deity
The glory of the nations
A light for all to see
That hope for all who will embrace His warm reality
Immanuel
Our God is with us
And if God is with us
Who could stand against us
Our God is with us – Immanuel[1]
- Immanuel, by Michael Card -

1.   Michael Card, 'Immanuel', The Promise. CD. 1991.

7

The Old Testament
in Three

Matthew 1:1-17

Some years ago my family moved to south London. We had lived in cities before, but never a city the size of London. For the first three weeks I drove around with a map on the seat next to me. A 300-page map of one city! The only way to learn my way around the area was to learn some landmarks: the office, the supermarket, church, home. Gradually I was able to move beyond the few roads between these landmarks and become comfortable driving around without the map.

Matthew launches the New Testament with something of a map. It is a set of three highlights to help us know where we are now in the New Testament, and where we've been in the Old Testament. At least four thousand years in almost a thousand chapters of Hebrew Scripture. Then after four hundred years of heavenly silence marked only by a blank page, we come to the fulfilment of all that has gone before: Jesus, the Christ!

Bible readers often lose heart when they see a genealogy. A long list of hard to pronounce names, this is hardly the most thrilling ingredient in the mix of God's inspired canon! Perhaps that is true, but this one, at least, is rather special. Matthew begins with a summary, ends with a summary and shapes the entire genealogy around three landmarks.

Matthew begins by telling the reader that Jesus is the son of David, the son of Abraham (v. 1). Then he leads us from Abraham through to David, from David through to the Exile and from the Exile through to Jesus, the Christ (vv. 2-16). Finally, to help us with our counting, he summarises the list as being three sets of fourteen generations between Abraham, David, Exile and Christ.

(If you are like me, you might be tempted to count the generations and find that there is an inconsistency in Matthew's mathematics ... what is going on? He obviously is trying to offer simplified shape, just as he is selectively including and excluding some generations in the genealogy. Remember this is a landmark map, not a satellite image of history in all its detail!)

There are all sorts of folk listed here: Isaac, Jacob and Judah – three generations of a very dysfunctional family from Genesis; godly men like Boaz and Josiah; significant characters like Jesse and Solomon; and most bizarrely, several key women (they are so important they'll get a chapter to themselves in this book!)

But the real focus needs to be on the three landmarks that Matthew's structure and his additional comments point us toward: Abraham, David, Exile.

ABRAHAM

Matthew could have chosen to begin his genealogy with Adam rather than Abraham. After all, Luke's genealogy goes back to Adam. In fact, Matthew seems to be structuring his genealogy around three landmarks that point toward divine promises. Each of these promises was a development of the original promise declaring the gospel to Adam and Eve: that the seed of the woman would come and crush the head of the serpent (Gen. 3:15). So Matthew gives us three landmarks in God's great salvation plan, each one tied to covenantal developments of the initial declaration of the gospel.

After the stage setting of Genesis 1-11, with humanity in rebellion against God, God called one man and made some extravagant promises to him (Gen. 12:2-3, 7). He would give him a land and innumerable seed, and He would bless all the families of the world through him. After humanity had tried to gain renown and make a name for themselves, God promised to make Abraham's name great. God's promise and subsequent covenant with Abraham marked him out as the starting point in a long line of divine faithfulness (see Gen. 15 for the covenant ceremony).

How would God bless all the families of the earth through Abraham's seed? And what if his descendants proved to be unfaithful, would the covenant be voided? God's covenant promise to Abraham was built on the solid and sure foundation of two words: 'I will!' God said it, that settles it. Despite the mess of his family line, despite the sin and failure of so many in the genealogy, God remained faithful to His promise.

Consider briefly the progression. Abraham's immediate descendants were significantly dysfunctional, but God kept restating the promise. Moses led the nation out of Egypt into the wilderness, where they were unfaithful to God. After Joshua had led them into the land, they were unfaithful to God. The period of the Judges was a spiraling disaster of unfaithfulness. Perhaps God should go quiet and let people forget the promise? Not at all, He added to it!

David

King David conquered Jerusalem, brought the ark of the covenant to the city, finished his palace and wanted to build God a house to replace the centuries-old tent. But God sent the prophet back to David to tell him that he would not build God's house, his son would. But God would actually build David a house, a dynasty (2 Sam. 7 & 1 Chron. 17). David's seed would reign on his throne forever!

Some of that promise would be fulfilled by Solomon, but not entirely. David was amazed. How could it be that God would establish his throne, not only over the nation, but over all of humanity? He looked back at all that God had done already, and he looked forward trying to imagine what this would all look like.

If David could have seen into the future, he would have been disappointed by much of what followed. His son gave his heart away to foreign wives and their gods. The nation divided. The throne of David was diminished, not enlarged. For generations the faithful would watch the Davidic king in despair, wondering when the seed of David, his greater son, would finally come. But eventually the final king was deposed and the throne lay in ruins.

The faithlessness of the people was now made worse by the faithlessness of their kings. Surely now God would go quiet and hope that people would forget the promises to Abraham and David? Absolutely not, He added to the promise!

Exile

The culmination of the infidelity of the people was the exile. To be taken away from the promised land, away from the temple, away from the place of blessing, away from God's territory – it was a national disaster! Yet God had predicted this. He had described it in the time of Moses, and after the nation divided He diligently sent prophets to cry out for Him. The reference to the Exile is like a shorthand pointer to the prophets.

Every prophet in our Bibles is either considered pre-exilic, exilic or post-exilic: that is, they all ministered before, during or after the exile. Their ministry was powerful but often apparently fruitless. They called on the people to turn, turn, turn back to the God who had made promises to Abraham and David. They called on the people to trust in the LORD and not in their own self-protection schemes. They warned of the coming discipline at the hands of evil Gentiles. Human sin must lead to divine judgment!

But on the black backdrop of sin and judgment, the prophets also offered the glimmering hope of God's grace spilling out in precious promises. God not only called them back to faith in past promises to Abraham and David, He added to the promise-plan!

In the future God would make a New Covenant. This New Covenant would provide for the full pardon of sin, it would replace dead stony hearts with living hearts and it would take the Law from external code in stone and write it on the hearts of the people. This New Covenant would give the fullness of fellowship with God that all people could know the LORD, with the requisite hope of restored divine life by the giving of the Spirit.

Surely now the people would turn to God and trust? Well, actually, no. They went into exile. They were brought back, but the return was not the glorious future they had expected. Hope was still offered, but the people descended again. The Old Testament ends with a faithless wimper, but with God's faithfulness still held out for the future. Four hundred years of silence and a blank page in our Bibles, but one thing is certain: the story was not finished.

Human failure, divine promise, our faithlessness, His loyalty, greater sin, greater promise...Abraham, David, New Covenant, what next? Jesus, the Christ!

Judah the father of Perez and Zerah by Tamar ...
and Salmon the father of Boaz by Rahab,
and Boaz the father of Obed by Ruth ... And David
was the father of Solomon by the wife of Uriah.
- Matthew 1:3-6 -

God of God,
Light of Light,
Lo! he abhors not the Virgin's womb:
Very God,
Begotten, not created;
O Come let us adore Him, Christ the Lord. [1]
- O Come All Ye Faithful -

The divine Son became a Jew; the Almighty appeared
on earth as a helpless human baby, unable to do
more than lie and stare and wriggle and make noises,
needed to be fed and changed and taught to talk like
any other child ... The more you think about it, the
more staggering it gets. [2]
- J. I. Packer -

---

1.   John F. Wade, 'O Come All Ye Faithful.' Ca. 1743.

2.   J. I. Packer, *Knowing God* (IVP, 1973), p. 53.

8

Ladies in Line?

Matthew 1:1-17

Matthew launches his Gospel and the New Testament with his highlights map of the Old Testament. Abraham, David, the Exile. God's great promises despite man's great failures. The three sets of fourteen(ish) generations include a whole host of people: patriarchs and kings, shepherds and farmers, good men and bad. But the most surprising inclusion of all those listed in the line of Jesus? The women.

WOMEN? HIGHLY UNUSUAL.

Tamar – The family of Abraham was dysfunctional at many levels. His great-grandson Judah left home and married a Canaanite woman. Their three sons developed their own soap-opera family saga involving Tamar, the wife of Er and then Onan. When Judah didn't honour the system and give his third son to Tamar to sire a son, she took matters into her own hands. Dressing as a cult prostitute, she engaged Judah himself in a liaison that led to her pregnancy. Indignant Judah was ready to have her put to death until his identification was brought out to prove his role in the matter. His conclusion? 'She is more righteous than I!' (Gen. 38:26)

Rahab – Some centuries later the people of Israel were entering the Promised Land. The two spies found a woman responsive to God in the person of Rahab. She proved to be faithful to God, protecting the spies and receiving divine deliverance when the Israelites came against Jericho. Matthew tells us that she was the 'mother' of a certain Boaz, a profoundly godly man of integrity (even if there were intervening generations so he never actually bounced on her knee). She has a place in the Hebrews 11 'Hall of Faith' and is listed alongside Abraham as James discusses how true faith leads to real works. So Rahab is known as Rahab the righteous, right? Uh, no. She will carry the label of Rahab the prostitute into eternity, but in heaven she is a heroine of the faith!

Ruth – Speaking of righteous women, surely Ruth is almost in a league of her own. Returning from Moab with Naomi in the days when the judges judged and everyone was doing what was right in his own eyes, Ruth proved to have a greater grip on God's kind of loyal love than the vast majority of God's own people. And God was faithful to this woman of faith. Despite her mother-in-law's attempts to force a marriage of promiscuous necessity with Boaz,

Ruth ends up with her reputation intact as Boaz makes sure their marriage is completely above board. Who ever would have thought that a Moabite widow could become the great grandmother of King David!

Mrs. Uriah – Speaking of King David – the man after God's own heart, the man who ruled Israel and brought to an end all the warfare, the man who is lauded and honoured above almost any other Old Testament hero of the faith. Speaking of King David, why is it that when his life is remembered there is an ugly stain included? David's mighty men were listed in 2 Samuel 23. Thirty-seven in all, with stories told of the feats of several. And if they were his men, what a man he must have been! And the final name to ring in the ears? Uriah the Hittite. Matthew doesn't let that incident drop either, listing Solomon's mother – not by name, but worse, as the one who had been Uriah's wife, Bathsheba, Mrs. Uriah. The lady spotted by a king who should not have been looking, and certainly should not have brought her into his palace. An illegitimate affair unsuccessfully covered by lies and murder. A stain on David's record, a thorn in the flesh of his family. Nonetheless, there she is, mother of Solomon, an ancestor of Jesus (see 2 Sam. 11–12).

So why did Matthew break with Jewish convention and include these four women in his genealogy of Jesus, the Christ? And if he was wanting to include women, why not Sarah, or Rachel, or Leah?

These women share four things that could make sense of their inclusion:

1. *They were all women.* I know, obvious in the extreme, but worthy of comment. Despite the reputation imposed on

Scripture as being misogynistic, yet again we see God's valuing of women alongside men. Both are equally valuable. Both are equally in need of a saviour.

2. They were all probably foreign. Tamar was likely a Canaanite or from Aram. Rahab was from pre-conquest Jericho. Ruth was a Moabitess. Mrs. Uriah was married to a Hittite. So if this is the reason that very Jewish Matthew includes the women it introduces an early hint to a later theme. In the next chapter we find non-Jewish Magi coming to visit the newborn king. By the end of the Gospel we grasp that Jesus wanted His followers to make disciples of all nations.

3. They all point to unusual divine providence. What lengths God seemed to go to in order to work out His great plan! He used the faithlessness of Judah to set up the line that would continue the promise. Who would have thought that an immoral hostess would turn out to be known beyond her generation in a conquered land? He even brought together a Moabite widow with good guy Boaz to prepare for the coming king. And a faithless liaison that shamed a king was used by God to lead to the greatest King. God's ways are not our ways. Surely the greatest King of all should have the most glorious of genealogies? Perhaps He does, if God's glory is a revelation of His grace!

4. They all had a huge question mark banner fluttering over their integrity. Tamar's incestuous act as a shrine prostitute raises all sorts of concerns. And Rahab may well be introduced even now in paradise as Rahab the, well, you know. Now Ruth was an exception since her integrity is underlined rather than undermined in the book that bears her name, but still, lying at the feet of a drunk man at night? I hear the banner flapping overhead. Then Mrs. Uriah, whether she had any choice or not, participated in an immoral adulterous tryst.

While there is something to be said for the first three commonalities, it is this last one that stands out above the rest. After all, there are five women in the genealogy, not four. Since Joseph was only Jesus' step-dad, his wife needed to be mentioned. Women in genealogies are unusual, but so is a virgin birth! So unusual, in fact, that Joseph and Mary would have to live with the wagging tongues and the fluttering question mark over her integrity for years to come. This 'virgin from Nazareth' was surely just a fraud. Or was she?

God didn't line up the arrival of His Son with a red carpet through the pages of the Old Testament. Instead the red line was that of the scarlet stain of sin. Far more imperfect people than paragons of virtue. Far more people like us than heroes in stained glass windows.

From people like us comes Jesus, the Christ, to people like us. God's grace overcoming the stain of sin!

'Behold, the virgin shall conceive and bear a son,
and they shall call his name Immanuel'
(which means, God with us).
- Matthew 1:23 -

The glory of the incarnation is that it presents to our
adoring gaze not a humanised God or a deified man,
but a true God-man – one who is all that God is
and at the same time all that man is: one on whose
almighty arm we can rest, and to whose human
sympathy we can appeal.[1]
- B.B. Warfield -

---

1.   Benjamin B. Warfield, *Selected Shorter Writings,* Vol.1 (Minnesota: Presbyterian & Reformed, 1970), p. 166.

9

We Do Not Face Sin Alone

Matthew 1:18-25

The genealogy of Matthew points to the fulfilment of the promises to Abraham and David. It also gets the reader thinking about the troubled reputation of several women in earlier days. Now we see another couple troubled by apparent sexual sin.

JOSEPH'S GRACIOUS PLAN (VV. 18-19)
Couples married young and this young couple had their lives before them. The young carpenter and his younger bride-to-be. But then the ultimate slap in the face: Joseph discovers that Mary is expecting a child. It is not hard to imagine the shattered dreams, repulsive images and the emotional turmoil that Joseph endured.

Not only did this crisis mean their forthcoming wedding was a sham, Joseph also now faced the shame of suspicion. The obvious pathway forward was to save face for himself by publically disgracing her and distancing himself. If he could be sufficiently indignant and distance himself, then maybe his honour could be saved. But Joseph did not choose the obvious path.

Public disgrace for Mary might have meant some sort of public execution by stoning, but even without that, public disgrace is too painful to describe in a shame and honour society. Joseph chose an incredibly gracious option: he would divorce her, and he would do so quietly. What would people say about him? The cloud of suspicion would linger, but Joseph looked out for the best interests of the girl who he thought had sinned. Joseph's selflessness is worthy of reflection, not least because we know what he didn't – the identity of the baby inside her!

GOD'S GREATER PLAN (vv. 20-21)

During the agonising turmoil of Joseph's deliberation, new information was introduced. Perhaps he tossed and turned on his bed. The thoughts, the images, the options, the consequences. But the troubled young man must have slept, for an angel of the Lord appeared in a dream.

He was told not to fear taking Mary into his home. He was told that the baby was in her from the Holy Spirit. He was told to name the boy Jesus. And he was told why.

Jesus. The Hebrew name Joshua. Yeshua in Aramaic. However we might pronounce it, this was a name of significance. Actually it was not unusual. There were lots of little Jesuses running around the neighbourhood for it was one of the most common boys' names in Palestine at that time. But the angel didn't just give the name choice, he also gave the reason. This boy would live up to His name – He would save people from their sins.

GOD'S GREAT PLAN PREDICTED (VV. 22-23)

Matthew adds some theological commentary for the sake of the reader. Going back to Isaiah 7:14, Matthew quotes the prophet's anticipation of a virgin giving birth to a special child with a special name. Ahaz may have been a king with all sorts of issues, but God was not out of touch with his struggling people. In fact, an unmarried woman was soon to give birth to a son of significance, and the significance was God's presence with the people.

What was true in Ahaz's day proved to be infinitely truer still with Mary. She was a virgin, unmarried, but with child. This time it was not a matter of sequencing prediction and then fulfillment by normal means. This time she truly bore a miracle child, a child whose significance could not be greater. Immanuel – God with us!

So what would Joseph do? Seems obvious: obey the angel. But not so fast. So he had insider information concerning the child inside her. The boy Jesus was to save the people from their sins and He would be God with us, Immanuel. All very well and perhaps worthy of some Christmas carols, but what about Joseph and Mary?

You can imagine his thinking. Two men come into his carpenter's shop and request a bid on a certain job. Joseph tells them a price. They look impressed but concerned. Joseph adds a comment about how they could trust his word. Little boy Jesus runs in and starts playing with some wood blocks. They look at the child and whisper to each other. Joseph hears a snippet of a comment about an angel in a dream. They laugh and press him further for assurance on whether he can follow through on his bid. Joseph knows what they are thinking. They leave and go looking for another carpenter, one they can trust.

The stigma of the sinful reputation would linger for years. It could cost them on so many levels. How would he provide for them? How would Mary cope with the dagger comments in the market? How long until the child sensed what everyone thought? It wasn't that nobody sinned in Nazareth, that was all too common. But when a couple perceived to be different turn out to be the same as everyone else, well, they don't get treated the same as everyone else. And what about family? What would they say? Family, friends, work and just about every aspect of life would be stained by the reputation of sinful infidelity.

JOSEPH'S IMMEDIATE OBEDIENCE (VV. 24-25)

Matthew leaves us with no doubt what kind of man Joseph was. He had been kind to Mary, even when he thought she had been unfaithful. And now he proved faithful to God when the days ahead looked so uncertain.

He took Mary into his home, thereby offering the protection and security she needed. A quick wedding was the best thing for all involved. Then he had no marital union with her until after she had the boy. And Joseph named the boy Jesus.

Three times Matthew points to the name of the child. Indeed, the significance of the birth story here is wrapped up in that name. Everyone thought they saw just a normal couple getting married in a hurry for the 'normal' reason and later giving birth to a son with a common name. But this was not normal in any way.

How could they face the uncertainties, the knowing looks, the suspicious smiles from family members, or worse, the rejection that may come their way? They could face the stigma of sin because this child was Jesus, the One who would save His people from their sin. This child was Immanuel, God with us.

Behold, wise men from the east came to Jerusalem,
saying, 'Where is he who has been born king of the Jews?
For we saw his star when it rose and have come to
worship him.'
- Matthew 2:1-2 -

It came without ribbons. It came without tags.
It came without packages, boxes or bags.
And he puzzled and puzzled 'till his puzzler was sore.
Then the Grinch thought of something he hadn't before.
What if Christmas, he thought, doesn't come from a store.
What if Christmas, perhaps, means a little bit more.[1]
- Dr. Seuss, *How the Grinch Stole Christmas* -

---

1. Dr. Seuss, *How the Grinch Stole Christmas* (New York: Random House, 1957).

10

The Expansive Power of a Foreign Collection

Matthew 2:1-12

Surprising visitors get your attention. At the start of Matthew's second chapter we are introduced to 'wise men from the east' who create a stir in the corridors of power in Jerusalem. Who were they and why did they show up?

THE MAGI

The Magi were highly educated priest-sages from somewhere east of Israel. They could have had Babylonian connections, travelled in from Arabia, or have been Persian. Some of the early church fathers identify them as Arabian (a place known for mining gold and growing both frankincense and myrrh). Other early traditions of the church identify them as Persian. In fact, when the Persians invaded the land of Palestine in

614, they left the Church of the Nativity in Bethlehem unharmed, because they saw the mosaic above the doorway had the Magi in Persian dress. While scholars can debate Arabian theories versus Persian theories, one fact is agreed by all: they were Gentiles.

Why do we refer to the Magi as 'three kings'? The 'three' assumes that it was one gift per person. We know they were more than one, but we do not know how many there were. But were they kings? Perhaps Psalm 72:10-11 is influential here in that the language of kings bearing gifts from Sheba will fit with the context, as we will see. But Matthew's account does not identify the visitors as kings, so we must stick with his account.

These men declared the reason for their journey: they had seen the new king's star. Perhaps a miraculous star-like light had led them all the way, not totally dissimilar to the foil-clad stars on sticks paraded around churches every time there's a nativity play. Or, more likely, they observed something profoundly stirring in the night sky.

Hebrew lore had long associated the coming Messiah with a star, because of Numbers 24:17: 'a star shall come out of Jacob, and a scepter shall rise out of Israel.' The Jewish anticipation of a coming king was no secret. The Roman historian Suetonius wrote, 'There had spread all over the East an old and established belief that it was fated for men coming from Judea at that time to rule the world.'[2] Communities of dispersed Jews in Mesopotamia could certainly have excited the local sky gazers with their ancient expectations.

---

2. Suetonius on Rulers from Judea: *Vespasianus IV*, quoted in Paul Maier, *In the Fullness of Time: A Historian Looks at Christmas, Easter and the Early Church* (Grand Rapids: Kregel, 1977), p. 50.

What Did the Magi See in the Sky?

With neither industrial nor light pollution, the ancient night sky was a familiar and fascinating stage with plenty of action to watch. While we may glance upwards now and then, they studied the skies very closely. Perhaps they saw a conjunction of planets that piqued their interest. Perhaps a comet grabbed their attention. Actually, it could well have been both.

The records show that Jupiter and Saturn converged in the constellation of Pisces in 7-6BC. Actually, Mars joined the party too a few months later, but stargazers might have struggled to see the third planet in the mix. Jupiter was the great king planet. Saturn was known as the shield, and was associated with Palestine (perhaps because of its connection with Saturday, and the Jews were the famous Sabbath observers). Pisces also had connections to this part of the world. So the convergence, combined with Hebrew lore, would have certainly grabbed their attention.

The next spring, March–April of 5BC, a comet known as Williams' new Comet number 52, would have been visible in the Middle East.[3] This confirmation probably got them on their camels and heading west to find this 'king of the Jews'.

So Where is the New King?

Unsurprisingly, the news of a new king did not thrill the corridors of power in Jerusalem. He was not born in Herod's palace (in fact, most of those who had been born to Herod were no more by this stage – more on Herod

---

3.   John Williams, *Observations of Comets from B.C. 611 to A.D. 1640 Extracted from the Chinese Annals* (London: Strangways and Walden, 1871), cited in Paul Maier, *In the Fullness of Time*, p. 342.

in the next chapter). So the experts were called, research undertaken and location identified. Bethlehem.

They quoted Micah 5:2 to the king, albeit with some adjustments. Bethlehem, now located in the land or district of Judah, is not to be considered insignificant. This would be a natural view of the place, but the explanation was given that a ruler is to come out of Bethlehem, one who will shepherd God's people Israel (this last bit pulled in from 2 Sam. 5:2).

Bethlehem was not the place you would naturally expect to find a child born to be king. Sure, it was the birthplace of King David, the shepherd turned king of God's people. But his kingly location would surely be Jerusalem, the throne city of the king! But perhaps political power was Herod's craving, whereas and this new King would be more in line with his ancestor David?

The Gentiles needed the Jewish scriptures to find the Christ, and they did. But the Jewish chief priests, although they had the scriptures, stayed in the city of power rather than running to the prophesied King.

So power-hungry Herod urged the Magi to find the child and report back to him. His motivations become clearer in the next section. The Magi left the king to go find the King.

The Gentiles Converge on the King!

In verses 9-12 we see the Magi following the star and arriving at a house in Bethlehem. Whatever astronomical wonder had stirred them to travel, the stellar signpost must now have been miraculous in some way, identifying the house where the child was. This brought about rejoicing with a joy great and exceeding – they were thrilled to be at their long-awaited destination.

Some will make much of their arriving at a house. Since we know that Jesus was born in a stable, this must mean they arrived a significant time after the birth. Combine this with the fact that Herod will later order the slaughter of male infants under two years of age, and suddenly we have a real problem with nativity plays – the Magi always arrive a couple of years too early! Or do they?

We do not know that Jesus was born in a stable. Reading the biblical account closely renders the stable an unlikely option for His birthplace. What we do know is that Mary and Joseph found no guest room in Bethlehem as all the guest rooms were already being used. The guest room was an addition to a humble house used for out of town guests. Perhaps we should shed our community motel image, and also shed our thoughts of well, the shed.

As we will see in Luke, when Jesus was born He was laid in a feeding trough. There, that proves it, a stable. Not so fast, detective. If you were a humble family in Bethlehem, would you entrust your two sheep and one donkey to a wooden stable standing vulnerably outside the village? Their security arrangements were not quite what we are used to these days. No, the typical arrangement would be to bring in the animals into a lower section of the living quarters for their overnight security and their family's central heating.

Jesus' birth was as humble as our image of a dilapidated stable, but with the added delight that He really did come to dwell among such as us. He was born humbly, laid in a manger, probably right in the living room of a very humble peasant home. And this is where the Magi came.

Jesus was born to be king, but not in a palace. He was likely born in a peasant's home - and not in the capital city, but a lowly village. Jesus was born to be king of all, not just the upper echelons of society. And as the camel-carried entourage of foreign dignitaries shuffled in, it became clear that this was not just a king for the Jews.

As Isaiah had written seven centuries before, the light of the glory of the LORD will dispel the darkness over all peoples. All peoples—the nations, the Gentiles, would come to His light (Isa. 60:3). Jesus is not only the king in the line of David (as we see in the Micah 5:2/2 Sam. 5:2 quotation), He is also in the line of Abraham (as we see all the families of the earth delighting in Him!). Here they were, a whole gang of Gentiles bringing gifts and bowing before the newborn king. Isaiah anticipated the future glories of the city of Jerusalem, but in Matthew we see the focus shifted from the city to the baby.

This entourage must have been quite the sight, bowing in their fine attire on a humble Judean floor. And as they do so, they expand for us the significance of Christmas. This was not just a local event, this was a global one. This was not just about the lower classes of society, but about rich Gentiles joining poor Jews. This was no longer private, for Jerusalem and the powers that be were waiting to hear more. And up above, even the stars of the cosmos were involved.

And then there were the gifts, perhaps expanding our understanding beyond theirs? Like the Queen of Sheba of old, here was a Gentile entourage bearing spices and very much gold for the Son of David (cf.1 Kings 10:2,10). Gold, the only gift worthy of a royal birth. Frankincense, a priestly fragrance reflecting the connection between this boy and the LORD of all. The combination of gold and frankincense, borne by camels, was also noted in Isaiah 60:6 as Gentiles converge on the light given by the LORD's glory arising upon His own.

But then there is one other gift. Myrrh. Precious, indeed, but what was its significance? A resin used in burial and death. Perhaps we will have to wait until eternity to ask how much they realised the significance of this gift . . . not a normal gift, but this was no normal King.

'A voice was heard in Ramah,
weeping and loud lamentation,
Rachel weeping for her children;
she refused to be comforted, because they are no more.'
- Matthew 2:18 -

The tremendous figure which fills the Gospels
towers in this respect, as in every other, above all the
thinkers who ever thought themselves tall. His pathos
was natural, almost casual. The Stoics, ancient and
modern, were proud of concealing their tears. He never
concealed His tears; He showed them plainly on His
open face at any daily sight, such as the far sight of
His native city.[1]
– G.K. Chesterton –

1.   G.K. Chesterton, *Orthodoxy* (Los Angeles: John Lane Company, 1909), p. 298.

11

Weeping Mother, Faithful Father

Matthew 2:13-18

Matthew's retelling of the birth of Jesus sandwiches two passages focused on unrighteous king Herod between three dreams of the righteous Jew, Joseph. Perhaps Herod lay awake at night fearfully concerned to protect his own position as king, while Joseph literally dreamed of the coming and protection of God's King!

Following the genealogy, the final section of chapter 1 presents the birth of Jesus, the son of David. The first part of chapter 2 underlines that this son of David was also the son of Abraham. Now we see again the truth that this child is, in fact, the son of God.

In six verses Matthew weaves together allusions to two momentous occasions in the history of Israel: the Exodus and the Exile. Two great persecutions of Israel. Two great deliverances by God. And now both converge in the personal history of God's Son Himself.

In this latter drama of the persecution and deliverance of God's Son, the 'son' is not Israel as a nation but the person of Jesus. And the evil enemy is neither Pharoah nor Nebuchadnezzar, but the evil tyrant Herod.

HEROD THE CHILD-KILLER

The playground bully is not excused by the complexities of his private life and personal insecurities, but he is often explained by them! Herod was exceedingly complex.

Racially he was an Arab, with an Idumean father and Nabatean mother. Yet religiously he was nominally Jewish. That is, his ancestors had been conquered and forcibly converted to Judaism by Hyrcanus, a Jewish ruler who then appointed Herod's grandfather as a governor. But culturally Herod was Greek. Not only was Greek his first language, but he tried to turn Jerusalem into a Greek city.

Politically, however, Herod was Roman. His father had strategically helped Julius Caesar and been handsomely rewarded. Herod followed in his father's footsteps and always sided with Rome, receiving his position during a visit to the capital of the empire. A personal friend of whoever had power, Herod masterfully negotiated the numerous shifts in Roman politics. For instance, as one who became a friend of Mark Antony, his position was surely under threat when Antony was defeated by Augustus. Yet by his scheming and negotiation skills, Herod managed to strengthen his position of power during a meeting with the new Caesar on the island of Rhodes.

Herod was powerful but paranoid. He led his army in ten different wars. He demonstrated his greatness by great architectural projects. The greatest achievement was the stunning temple in Jerusalem (to appease the Jews), but he started this project after many others that were less popular with the locals. He had funded and built temples in Gentile territories (to support the influence of Greek culture). He built himself a palace in Jerusalem, and further offended the Jews by introducing the five-yearly games in honour of Caesar. He re-established the seaport of Caesarea, also in honour of, well, Caesar (all to keep the Romans happy).

With such personal complexity and conflicting influences, it is not surprising that Herod's position of power felt so vulnerable. Like a child standing atop a great climbing frame, everyone else felt like a threat. Herod married ten women, but saw their children as threats to his position. He had three sons killed, as well as his favourite wife, Mariamne (and her grandfather, her mother, his brother-in-law, plus numerous subjects, including drowning the high priest, who was another of his brothers-in-law!)[2]. Augustus is said to have noted that he would rather be Herod's sow than his son, for it would have a greater chance of survival in a Jewish community (as in English, the difference between the words is a single letter).

When he finally died he even had a plan to generate mourning in the land. He had thousands of Jews arrested and detained in the stadium of Jericho. Upon his death they were to be slaughtered so that there would be mourning in the land. Fortunately, the order was not carried out.

JOSEPH THE CHILD-RESCUER

Joseph was again visited by an angel of the Lord to prepare him for the drama about to unfold. Again, the dream concerned Mary and the baby. Again there was reason to

---

2.   Paul Maier, *In the Fullness of Time* (Grand Rapids: Kregel, 1977), p. 64.

fear, but instruction to supersede that fear. This time the child was threatened with destruction by Herod. The Magi had left town and detoured away from Jerusalem. Joseph's journey south to Bethlehem would now involve a return with a detour even farther south, to Egypt!

A righteous father would go to any lengths to deliver his wife and child. The same is true here. Only the Father is actually God (don't forget chapter 1!). And so the section closes with a fulfilment formula – 'Out of Egypt I called my son!' (Hosea 11:1). God has done it again! Hosea is actually only looking back to the first deliverance of Israel from Egypt. He is not anticipating any future event. Is Matthew careless in his use of the Old Testament here? Not at all. He is clearly seeing the history of Israel relived in the person of Jesus. Matthew is seeing a 'filling up' of the idea of the original Exodus, this time in God's deliverance of His literal son from persecution and from Egypt.

So much is packed into so few verses, but we are only halfway through the section! Building on the Exodus imagery, Matthew now draws in the other great persecution and deliverance of the Old Testament: the Babylonian Exile.

HEROD'S FURY

If Herod's early years were characterised by his power and charm, his declining years were marked by his paranoia and brutality. He ended up dying with a painful disease that made him crave the escape of suicide, although he was thwarted. It takes no stretch of the imagination to imagine Herod's fury at being outwitted by the Magi and venting his fury and fears on the boys of Bethlehem. He had determined from the Magi when the star had arisen, which makes sense of why he killed every male child under the age of two years. This helps to date the birth of Jesus very late in the life of Herod, who died in April of 4BC.

Actually, in terms of Herod's sinister soap-opera of a life, the killing of a relatively low number of boys in Bethlehem would barely register in the annals of history.

RACHEL'S WOE

His brutality did register, of course, with every Jewish mother in Bethlehem and beyond. So the cry of lament rising from the little village of Bethlehem stirs a quote from Jeremiah 31:15—Rachel weeping for her children in Ramah, refusing to be comforted. Rachel, effectively the mother of the nation, was buried on the road to Bethlehem (Gen. 35:19). So now Matthew uses the ancient quote to paint a vivid image of the fresh grief of Jewish mothers at this local slaughter of innocents.

Is the quotation a tenuous link to the weeping of a Jewish mother? No, here is Matthew in his rich biblical brilliance! Why is Rachel described as weeping in Ramah? Ramah was not a reference to the area of Bethlehem, it was a specific location further north. In fact, 1 Samuel 10:2 specifies where Rachel was buried back in Genesis 35:19 – it was on the road to Bethlehem, yes; but specifically it was at Ramah. Ramah was later the hometown of Samuel (1 Sam. 28:3), but the significance in Jeremiah 31 comes much later than even Samuel's day.

In Jeremiah 31:15, the prophet is describing the grief of the nation as the sons are led away into exile. The prophet tells us that Ramah was a staging post on the journey from Judah to Babylon (Jer. 40:1-2). Brilliantly, Matthew builds on the Exodus image of Pharoah's slaughter of infants by shifting focus to the tears of mothers in the exile.

Jeremiah 31 makes the same shift. Earlier in the chapter the prophet used language from the Exodus to speak of God's future restoration of the nation—God's grace in the wilderness for those who survived the sword. Indeed, it is a theme of Jeremiah that God's future restoration of Israel from exile would eclipse God's deliverance in the Exodus (cf. Jer. 16:14-15; 23:7).

As in Hosea 11, Jeremiah 31:9 speaks of God being a father to the nation. Indeed, by verse 15 the future seems bleak. The sons are led away into exile, passing the tomb of Rachel the mother of Israel, who weeps because her sons are no more.

The Exodus and the Exile are woven powerfully into this section as Matthew describes the cry of lament from Bethlehem. But there is more!

God's Plan

Just as we need to look at the verses leading up to the Jeremiah quote, so we must also look beyond it. Matthew offers a drawer handle that should be pulled, revealing a wealth of delight beyond the despair of the moment. Through Jeremiah God urges the hopeless to hope in Him. In verse 20 God reiterates that He is a father to the nation.

Verse 26 reveals that Jeremiah was sleeping and dreaming pleasant dreams. From verse 27 to the end of the chapter we read of the great hope of Israel and Judah, a hope contrasted with and eclipsing the hope offered even in the Exodus. Rachel may weep in despair at the loss of her sons, but the loss is not forever. The passage is a passage of hope, for what God did in the Exodus will be surpassed by what God will do beyond the Exile. The tears of the Exile are coming to a conclusion with weeping in Bethlehem.

Why? What is the hope beyond the Exile? It is the New Covenant!

The New Covenant stands in the background of Herod's brutal act of infanticide? Indeed, for God's great plan is closer than ever as the despairing cry rises up from Bethlehem. Life has been tragically lost, and nothing can restore the lifeless sons in their mothers' arms. But God the Father has a plan for His Son Israel, a plan that will involve the brutal killing of His Son Jesus at the other end of Matthew's Gospel. And what will that achieve? It will bring in all the blessings of the New Covenant, not just for Israel and Judah, but for all nations ... sins forgiven, transformed hearts, personal relationship with God Himself!

Brutal King Herod was not in the line of David. Young Jesus was. And God His Father made sure to deliver His Son Jesus from the death of the innocents just as He promised to deliver His 'Son' Israel. And one day God the Father would deliver His Son Jesus to death as an innocent in order to bring about the hope of the New Covenant for many. Brutal King Herod. Faithful Father God.

And he went and lived in a city called Nazareth,
so that what was spoken by the prophets might be fulfilled,
that he would be called a Nazarene.
- Matthew 2:23 -

Christ is the cause of the greatest division,
but he is also the medium of the greatest union.[1]
- C.H. Spurgeon -

The supreme paradox must be this:
[Jesus] taught publicly for only three and one-half years.
He wrote no book. He had no powerful religious or
political machine behind him
—indeed, the ranking spiritual and governmental
authorities opposed him—and yet he became the
central figure in human history.[2]
- Paul Maier -

1.   C.H.Spurgeon, 'A Sermon Intended for Reading on Lord's Day, January 20, 1901.' Sermon 2710.31.

2.   Paul Maier, *In the Fullness of Time* (Grand Rapids: Kregel, 1977), p. 87.

12

God with Us, God Like Us: A Nazarene

Matthew 2:19-23

The flight to Egypt was short-lived. The aged tyrant Herod died shortly after the atrocity in Bethlehem. Yet again Joseph saw an angel in a dream, this time with instruction to return to Israel. As always, Joseph obeyed and so the family returned to Israel.

Yet things were not all well. Herod had died, but his replacement stirred fear within Joseph. So another dream directed him back to Galilee and the town of Nazareth. It took divine direction to return to Nazareth.

Joseph knew of the challenges facing the family in the town that thought it knew Joseph and Mary all too well. How would he rebuild his business when everyone thought they understood the truth about the circumstances surrounding Jesus' conception? How could Joseph gain respect when everyone doubted his word on this most important of issues? And how would Mary face the snickers and gossip that inevitably would accompany the return of 'the virgin' with her little boy?

So Joseph's initial plan was to return to Bethlehem and set up home there. They probably had family in the town. Furthermore, they had lived there for some months after the birth of Jesus. It would not take much work for him to support his new young family. But news of Herod's death was tempered by news of his replacement.

ANOTHER HEROD?

King Herod was never settled on who should succeed him. His six wills attest to that. On his deathbed he ordered the execution of one son, then changed his will again, appointing Archelaus in place of the older Antipas over the half of his kingdom that included Judea. Archelaus was like his father in respect to both personal vices and weaknesses, but lacked some of his father's political guile. Upon taking charge he ordered the slaughter of 3000 Jews at the Passover – those he deemed to be opponents and threats to his reign.

In light of this news, perhaps Galilee made sense to Joseph after all. Still, it took divine direction for him to head there and go back to Nazareth. This would not be easy, but it was God's plan.

There is a progression of locations in this short passage. Joseph is directed to Israel, the land of the Jews. Then he is directed to Galilee. This was also Jewish territory, but it had a high number of Gentiles and was scorned by the 'better Jews' of Judea. This was 'Galilee of the Gentiles'. So Matthew again reinforces the notion that this Messiah was not just for the Jews, but for the Gentiles too. In fact, with His growing up in Nazareth, we will see that He was for all of us.

THE PLACE OF NO GOOD THING: NAZARETH
After this section, Nazareth is mentioned three more times in Matthew's Gospel. In chapter 4:13-16 it is mentioned in association with other Galilean towns as the place of darkness wherein a great light dawned, the region of Galilee of the Gentiles.

In chapter 21:11, the city of Jerusalem was stirred by the triumphal entry of this Jesus, so they asked the crowds who He was. The crowds (probably largely Galilean in composition as they were arriving on that side of town) replied that this was the prophet Jesus, specifically the one from Nazareth in Galilee. This answer may not have thrilled the Jerusalem folk!

Finally in 26:71, Peter was in the courtyard of Annas' house when a servant girl saw him and identified him as an accomplice of Jesus of Nazareth. Was there any venom in that label? Probably, since Peter was again confronted, this time betrayed by his Galilean accent. To be from Nazareth was not a positive in Judea. In fact, it was not a good thing, even in Galilee!

Nazareth was five miles from Sepphoris, the strongest military centre in Galilee. It was on a branch of the great caravan route to Damascus. For traders, soldiers and travellers, Nazareth was just a rest stop on the way to somewhere better.

Essentially, Jesus grew up in Nowhere, Galilee. Was this the next best thing since God's plan A (Bethlehem) had been thwarted by troublesome Herodian rulers? Not at all. God directed Joseph so that Mary was brought back to Nazareth, and Jesus was brought up in Nazareth. This meant that the Messiah born in Bethlehem would always be called the Nazarene.

THE PROPHETS FULFILLED

So which Old Testament passage is being fulfilled here? This has caused some consternation among scholars. Where does the Old Testament say the Messiah will be raised in Nazareth? Nowhere. But somehow Matthew points to fulfilment in Jesus being a Nazarene. It is worth noting that Matthew here refers to the prophets, plural. Perhaps several options should be combined to get a composite sense of Matthew's subtlety here:

Jesus was, perhaps, to be considered a Nazirite (*Nazir*)—a chosen holy one set apart for God's service from His mother's womb, just like Samson the deliverer (Judg. 16:17; note also that the divine/angelic announcement to Samson's parents referred to his 'saving Israel'); and Samuel the priest (note the parallels between Mary's song and Hannah's song in Luke 1).

Furthermore, Jesus was the Messianic 'branch' (*Neser*)—the Davidic branch of Jeremiah 23:5 and 33:15, who would reign in righteousness over the earth; the branch who would rebuild the temple and bear royal honour in Zechariah 6:12; the branch from Jesse's stump anticipated in Isaiah 11:1 as part of the great royal Immanuel section.

Perhaps instead of choosing one over the other we have two of Matthew's great themes converging: for again, Matthew weaves together priest and king in the description of the deliverer Jesus. Again, Matthew brings us back to Isaiah's Immanuel prophecy with which he began his sequence of fulfilments at the end of chapter 1.

Joseph called His name Jesus in chapter 1, and by the end of chapter 2 it is Joseph that brings Him to Nazareth so that all would call Him a Nazarene. This child, the son of Abraham, the son of David, the son of God, is to be known by all people, forever, as Jesus the Nazarene!

But was Matthew more directly and deliberately pointing to a location, rather than pointing the reader toward the subtlety inherent in the name itself? Indeed he was, for every Old Testament citation in this second chapter pointed to a geographical location: Bethlehem, an allusion to 'the nations', Egypt, Ramah, and now, Nazareth.

Perhaps another Old Testament reference can come into play here – Isa.53:2. This offers no reference to geography, but uses the associated terminology of 'a root' in underlining the lowliness and obscurity of this holy priest-king.

A REPUTATION WORTH CARRYING?

Jesus knew the life of the poor (as seen in His parables of sowing and reaping, sparrows, children at weddings and funerals, women grinding at the mill, etc.). Jesus experienced the fullness of human life and society. He was not sheltered in some rich ivory tower, protected from the 'dross of society'. He lived in the midst of it all, and He carried it as His label.

Jesus was a very common name at that time, so He needed an identifier. Who was His Dad? That was complicated. What was His job? Again, not easy. So where was He from? Nazareth became the label so often appended to His name.

In the only childhood glimpse of Him we see Jesus leaving behind a child-prodigy role in the temple to live in submission to His parents in Nazareth (Luke 2:51).

At the start of His ministry, when Philip wanted to introduce Nathanael to Jesus, he used the Nazareth label. The guile-less Nathanael replied with a sarcastic question: 'can anything good come out of Nazareth?' (John 1:45-6). Jesus returned from His base in Capernaum to His hometown synagogue in Nazareth, where His reading of Isaiah and commentary on some Gentiles being blessed in the Old Testament received a warm reception, in both senses of the term (Luke 4:16). His subsequent visit to a synagogue in Capernaum sees Him identified as Jesus of Nazareth by an unclean spirit, who also acknowledges that He is the Holy One of God. Jesus accepts the label, but silences the spirit once His heavenly identity is declared (Mark 1:24-25; Luke 4:34-35).

As His ministry progressed, down south near Jericho, blind Bartimaeus hears that Jesus of Nazareth is nearby and launches into loud pleading toward the Son of David (Mark 10:47; Luke 18:37-38).

At His arrest, John describes the dignified Jesus walking out to meet the arresting party. Who is it they are looking for? Jesus of Nazareth. Jesus' response 'I am He,' declares both His divine identity (this repeated 'I Am' statement, concludes the lesser known sequence of 'absolute I Am's' in John's Gospel). At the same time he does not shy away from the geographical label. 'I am He'(18:5).

During His trial Jesus' label was used disparagingly of Peter in the courtyard of Annas' house (see also Mark 14:67). In his death, John's record has Pilate's inscription identifying the 'criminal' as 'Jesus of Nazareth, the King of the Jews'.

After His resurrection the two disconsolate disciples on the road to Emmaus refer to Jesus as being 'of Nazareth' (Luke 24:19). Fair enough, their hopes had been dashed.

But we also read of the very angel in the tomb itself using the label! Surely an angel sent from God could come up with a better label!? (See Mark 16:6)

Even after His ascension Jesus continues to bear the lowly label 'of Nazareth'. Peter's presentation of Pentecost culminates with Jesus as both Lord and Christ, but it launches with Jesus of Nazareth (Acts 2:22). The lame man is healed, not in the name of the risen and ascended Christ, but in the name of Jesus of Nazareth (Acts 3:6; 4:10). Stephen's accusers refer to Jesus of Nazareth (Acts 6:14). Peter declares to Gentiles that God anointed and was with Jesus of Nazareth (Acts 10:38). Then we discover that Jesus used the label of Himself when He appeared to Paul on the road to Damascus (Acts 22:8)! This had been the name opposed by Paul in his days of Christian persecution (Acts 26:9), and indeed even Jesus' followers had to bear the disparaging label (Acts 24:5).

God was with this Jesus of Nazareth. And in His willingness to carry this label in ministry up north and down south, in His arrest, His crucifixion, His resurrection and even in His ascension, this Jesus of Nazareth was most assuredly 'with us'.

Immanuel, God with us. Not just near us, in some nice palace somewhere. But with us, like 'in Nazareth' with us. Jesus of Nowhere, Galilee. He came to be with us, so that He could be for us. And He is forever with us, for He still carries the lowliest of labels. It was all part of God's plan, that He should be called a Nazarene.

PART THREE:

The Presence of Peace in Person

Luke 1–2

*Inasmuch as many have undertaken to compile
a narrative of the things that have been accomplished
among us, just as those who from the beginning were
eyewitnesses and ministers of the word have delivered
them to us, it seemed good to me also, having followed
all things closely for some time past, to write an
orderly account for you, most excellent Theophilus,
that you may have certainty concerning the things
you have been taught.*
- Luke 1:1-4 -

*Luke was not only a Doctor, and a historian, but he
was one of the world's greatest men of letters. He wrote
the clearest and the best Greek written in that century.
… without Luke, we never could have had a report
from a competent man of science on the birth from
a Virgin. If Jesus had two human parents, why did the
shrewd Gentile Physician never suspect that fact?[1]*

- John A. Scott, *We Would Know Jesus* -

---

1.   John A. Scott, *We Would Know Jesus* (Abingdon, 1939), p. 130, cited by
      Wilbur M. Smith, *The Supernaturalness of Christ* (2011), p. 100.

13

The Truth
of the Incarnation

Luke 1:1-4

Christmas is a season of iconic images: the snow-covered stable, the audience of quiet animals, the contented couple. It can so easily take on the feel of a legend, the stuff of myth. But is it just a fairy tale? Is it a nice sweet way to launch the career of a significant character? Or is it true?

Certainly there are elements of the standard Christmas card images that may be some distance from the reality of the birth of the Christ. But Luke goes out of his way to underline that he is dealing with facts when he writes his Gospel. In an age of scepticism and relativism, we cannot afford to ignore the launch of his Gospel.

Jesus' life, ministry, death and resurrection caused a significant stir. As a result many sought to write down some sort of account. Luke decided it was right for him to do likewise. Yet as he launches into his account of the life of Christ, he wants to make sure his reader, Theophilus, knows his standards.

FIRST, HE USES THE BEST OF SOURCES

When you are dealing with the retelling of events, you cannot beat eyewitnesses. Luke's source for his material is that of the eyewitness: those who were there and saw it all for themselves. And he doesn't rely on just one, he did his research over a period of time pursuing accounts from multiple eyewitnesses.

Paul tells us that Luke was a physician, and a beloved one too (Col. 4:14). The evidence of both his Gospel and Acts support this designation. Luke includes all sorts of details about ailments and physical conditions. Furthermore, it isn't hard to image Dr Luke, with his caring bedside manner, drawing out the facts from such eyewitnesses as Mary, the mother of Jesus.

So Luke took his time and diligently researched. And he wanted his reader to know, from the very beginning, that his sources were reliable. He had used eyewitness testimony, no less – from those who were there at the very beginning of it all – i.e. before the birth of Jesus.

SECOND, HE PRODUCES THE BEST OF ACCOUNTS

Most scholars agree that Mark's Gospel was used as the base for both Matthew and Luke. But Luke's Gospel is not simply Mark-plus. It is carefully crafted into what Luke describes as an 'orderly account'.

He begins at the beginning and flows through to end at the end, which Acts shows was actually just the beginning of all that Jesus was doing in the world. Luke's structure follows an orderly and largely linear progression, giving the sense of progress from birth to ministry in Galilee through the journey to Jerusalem, to culminate in the Passion and Ascension of the risen Christ.

THIRD, HE INTENDS FOR THE BEST OF RESULTS

Why did Luke write his Gospel? He was not in the hunt for literary awards, although he surely deserves awards for accuracy of research and care in writing. He wrote so that Theophilus might have certainty concerning the things he had been taught.

The reliable eyewitnesses, the careful research, the orderly account, all work together to produce certainty for the reader. We do not know who Theophilus was. Perhaps he was an acquaintance of Luke, some have suggested the trial lawyer for Paul, others that the name implies a generic reader – any 'God-lover' who might care to read.

Whoever he was, we can sit in his place and read Luke's account. Our experience can be the same, to find certainty concerning the life and times of Jesus. More than that, to respond with love for the God who stepped into our world that first Christmas.

IN THE PRESENCE OF TWO WITNESSES…

Luke does not simply affirm his reliability in the introductory verses. He proceeds to reinforce his reliability by carefully offering pairs of witnesses throughout his Gospel. In the ancient law court a fact was established if two reliable witnesses would attest to it. With a forceful subtlety Luke brings in his witnesses two-by-two.

Consider the opening pair of chapters: the angel Gabriel visits and speaks twice – to Zechariah and then to Mary. The response of the angelic visit recipients is seen in two magnificent songs – Mary's *Magnificat,* and Zechariah's *Benedictus.* The name of John is confirmed by two witnesses – his mother and then his father. The timing of Jesus' birth is located by two historical timeframes – Caesar Augustus' decree and the governership of Quirinius in Syria. The birth of the second boy is affirmed by both his parents and the angelically informed shepherd-witnesses. And these shepherd-witnesses (a strange choice in the ancient world), went away praising God for all they had both seen and heard. Then Jesus is taken to the temple where He receives testimony from two special saints. And just to finish the section off, we have Jesus back in the temple for the second time in His childhood, again impressing those present.

Luke continues using pairs throughout his Gospel. Often he will use both a male and a female side-by-side: consider the story of the lost sheep paired with the story of the lost coin as preparation for the story of the two lost sons. But his carefully crafted witness upon witness style comes to the fore again in the final two chapters.

We find Pilate repeatedly affirming Jesus' innocence, yet paired with Herod in mistreating and condemning him. Then Jesus is crucified between two criminals, one of whom rightly saw the unique innocence of Jesus. Both the centurion and the crowds were stunned by the manner of His death. His body was buried by Joseph of Arimathea, with the women offering the second witness to the site of the burial. Two angels attested to His resurrection, which was then told a second time by the women to the disciples. Peter had to see for himself, and having run to the tomb he saw both the linen cloths lying separated. Two disciples walked to Emmaus and encountered the risen Christ together, who offered a lesson in Old Testament studies from both the books of Moses and the books of the Prophets. Jesus appeared twice in Luke's account, offering the evidence of both His hands and feet.

Luke wants his reader to know the certainty of the things taught about Jesus. His piling up of paired witnesses attests to the reliability of his account. He wants the reader to know the certainty of the birth of Christ, and he wants his reader to grasp the certainty of the death and resurrection of Christ. For Luke, these two great moments in history are too important to let slip into the category of myth or legend.

*'Do not be afraid, Zechariah, for your prayer has
been heard, and your wife Elizabeth will bear you
a son, and you shall call his name John. And you
will have joy and gladness, and many will rejoice at
his birth, for he will be great before the Lord. And he
must not drink wine or strong drink, and he will be
filled with the Holy Spirit, even from his mother's
womb. And he will turn many of the children of Israel
to the Lord their God, and he will go before him
in the spirit and power of Elijah, to turn the hearts
of the fathers to the children, and the disobedient to
the wisdom of the just, to make ready for the Lord
a people prepared.'*
– Luke 1:13-17 –

*Alongside these cosmic, national, and salvific themes
is the simple personal story of Zechariah and
Elizabeth. They were a righteous, childless couple
who prayed for a child. God visited them and heard
their prayer of pain. … Scripture reveals requests
answered immediately, requests answered eventually,
and requests denied for a better way. In this case,
the answer to a personal prayer comes after years of
waiting and calls forth a response of praise.*[1]
– Darrell L. Bock –

---

1.   Darrell Bock, *Luke: Baker Exegetical Commentary on the New Testament*
      (Grand Rapids: Baker, 1994), p. 100.

14

If I Could Just Say Three Things

Luke 1:5-25

When the elderly priest stumbled out of the temple that afternoon he was bursting to say three things, but he could not say a word. This was not a dramatic individual feigning speechlessness, this was angelic discipline for disbelief. Nevertheless, even though his vocal cords had been unplugged, his heart was electrified. He was fit to burst, and just over nine months later it would all come out, but that comes later in the chapter.

Zechariah and Elizabeth were an elderly and godly couple, faithful to God's commands and blameless, long-time servants in the priestly division of Abijah. For most of the year this meant service in the Judean hills. But twice a year, for a week, Zechariah's division was on duty in

Jerusalem. These were busy weeks, but a real delight for a faithful servant like Zechariah.

Luke's Gospel begins with Zechariah receiving the opportunity of a lifetime – being selected by lot to tend the altar of incense. With 800 priests in each division, this was a lottery that could pass you by completely. For years Zechariah had heard the lot falling to another priest. Then this day it fell to him. At 3pm, with the crowds waiting outside, Zechariah walked as far into the temple as any human could go.

He left behind the Court of the Woman and the Court of Israel (the limits for women and men, respectively). He crossed the area reserved for priests, passed the altar, passed the golden sea, over the threshold and past the candlesticks on his left. He walked past the table of showbread on his right and proceeded toward the giant curtain separating the Holy Place from the Most Holy Place. Only the High Priest could go through that curtain, and that only once a year. Just this side of the curtain stood the altar of incense, Zechariah's goal.

Zechariah did not have a personal passion for burning incense, or if he did, that was not what made this privilege so wonderful. His passion was for the presence of God, and from his perspective getting within feet of the Most Holy Place was just that: getting close to the presence of God.

With his heart pounding he would have poured the incense on to the coals. The smoke would have risen up before him, representing the prayers of the nation, the prayers of saints like him. Perhaps the smoke stung his eyes. Certainly his heart pounded as he sought to get it just right. Then, suddenly, in the shadows cast by his body to the right of the altar, stood an angel of the Lord!

Talk about heart-stopping! Surely this could mean nothing but judgment for some oversight on his part. In fact, fear so gripped him that it is no wonder the angel began with that sure-fire sign of angelic presence: 'Do not be afraid!' While that opener may be expected of angelic visits, the next line surely caught Zechariah's attention. 'Your prayer has been heard.'

As the smoke rose before the aged priest, the visitor from heaven assured him that his prayers rose to God. More than that, God *heard* his prayer. Which prayer? The prayer he had prayed as he approached the altar of incense? Would it not be thrilling if it turned out that the aged priest had actually been drawn by lot twice? Perhaps as a young married man he had approached the altar and prayed for his wife and future children. Perhaps decades later he discovered that prayer had been heard? This is highly unlikely. Some scholars suggest the privilege of tending the altar of incense was restricted to once in a lifetime, which would make such speculation impossible. Nonetheless, when Zechariah stumbled out of the temple minutes later, three truths were bursting to come out of his frozen voice box:

1. I Am Going to be a Dad!

Perhaps the prayer that had been heard was not the prayer of a specific moment in time, but the prayer of a lifetime. The prayer prayed in anticipation of marrying his sweetheart, Elizabeth. The prayer of expectation prayed in the early weeks of marriage. The prayer of concern prayed as the months turned into years without a tiny newcomer to the home, with all the added pressures of a culture quick to shame the childless. The prayer of desperation as barren Elizabeth cried herself to sleep on his shoulder at night. The prayer of resignation as the years passed and a later phase of life dawned for them both. That prayer. The prayer of a lifetime. The prayer of a hopeful, then hurting couple.

That prayer had been heard. And now he and Elizabeth would have a baby boy – talk about joy!

Surely that would have been the first thing he'd want to talk about, but his question of the angel stirred a fiery response from Gabriel. Ever the announcer of great news relating to the nation of Israel, Gabriel was not to be taken lightly, or even questioned with doubt. Gabriel had been with God, had been sent by God and spoke representing God. Not good to doubt God! Thus he would be dumbstruck at just the time he wanted to speak like never before. He had so much to say.

Not only was he going to be a dad, but the next thing was even more amazing:

2. My Son Really is Going to be Special!

Of course, every parent thinks their child is special. He understands so much, she got her first tooth in record time, he is in the 99th percentile, she walked at nine months, etc. Yes, every child is special, but Zechariah's son was extra special. No, really.

For one thing, he would be great before the Lord. He would be set apart in a Nazirite-like dedication to God, not just for a season of early zealous adulthood, but lifelong. He would be filled with the Spirit of God, not just for a season of special ministry, but from his mother's womb. This was a special boy alright!

In fact, by verse 16 Gabriel had begun quoting language Zechariah would surely have recognised. It was the language of Malachi 4:5-6, the final words of the written prophets. Somehow this little boy would grow to be an Elijah-like prophet: he would bring about relational restoration on a horizontal level (fathers and children), and vertically (disobedient to the godly ways). It was also the language of Malachi 3:1, the anticipation of a coming preparer – one who would prepare the way, which would literally mean preparing the people, as in Gabriel's words. Zechariah knew that his son would be the last and greatest of the Old Testament prophets, set apart by heaven for a unique work of preparation! But even that was not the greatest thing on his heart, there was one more thing Zechariah was bursting to proclaim:

3. GOD IS COMING!
If his boy would be the Elijah-like prophet preparing the way, then Malachi was crystal clear who the way was for! This boy, John, would be preparing the way for me, declares the LORD. 'The Lord whom you seek will suddenly come to his temple ...' No need to beat around the bush here. If Malachi's great messenger was coming to prepare the way, then that could mean only one thing. The Lord Himself was soon coming to His temple!

But Zechariah could say nothing. He could only motion with wild hands and eyes transfixed. The people got that he had seen a vision, but they did not get the half of it!

For the next months only Elizabeth knew what was going on. She could feel John kick and elbow, she could see Zechariah smiling silently, the scroll of Malachi stretched out on their table, the look of wonder still in his aging eyes. While he could not say a word yet, Elizabeth could. 'Thus the Lord has done for me in the days when he looked on me, to take away my reproach among people' (Luke 1:25). God had heard the prayer of this godly lady, for he stoops to look far down, giving the barren woman a home, making her the joyous mother of children, praise the LORD! (Ps. 113:6, 9).

*In the sixth month the angel Gabriel was sent from
God to a city of Galilee named Nazareth, to a virgin
betrothed to a man whose name was Joseph, of the
house of David. And the virgin's name was Mary.
And he came to her and said, 'Greetings, O favoured
one, the Lord is with you!'*
– Luke 1:26-28 –

*God did not derive his divinity from Mary;
but it does not follow that it is therefore wrong to say
that God was born of Mary....
She is the true mother of God....
Mary suckled God, rocked God to sleep,
prepared broth and soup for God, etc.*[1]

– Martin Luther, *On the Councils and the Church* –

---

1.   Martin Luther, *On the Councils and the Church* in Luther's Works vol. 41,
     pp. 93-106.

15

Gabriel Visits Mary

Luke 1:26-56

His mission to an elderly and faithful priest in the temple looked like an ideal trip for majestic Gabriel. Announcing the coming of the long-awaited preparatory prophet to a godly man in God's house. But then his next mission must have caused some angelic head-scratching: to be sent to a nobody in a nothing-good town, to announce the birth of the Lord Himself? Surely even angels have been perplexed by God's great plan throughout the ages!

Nazareth was not a town with a great reputation. With traders passing through and Roman soldiers garrisoned locally, the notion of a virgin in Nazareth was almost laughable. But there was one. A young teenager named Mary. Gabriel arrived with a flourish, 'Greetings, O favoured one, the Lord is with you' (Luke 1:28)! She was greatly troubled. She may well have remained troubled throughout the centuries as many continue to misunderstand her unique role.

Is Mary the wonderful woman who offers an approachable side to a distant and frightening God? Not according to Mary. Surely this is her account through Luke's pen, and the emphasis is the very opposite of her own greatness. She was a nobody. Certainly she was a godly young lady, but she was humble, poor, unimpressive. And yet she had been chosen by God to bear the very approachability of God Himself, His Son.

A GREATER MIRACLE THAN THE VIRGIN BIRTH

Of course, the virgin conception and birth was a great miracle, but the greater miracle was who the child was inside her. Another miracle son, but this one surpassed John before him. John was to be great in the sight of the Lord. This boy would be great in Himself. Typically this kind of descriptor had been used of God in the books of the Old Testament.

This would be the Son of the Most High, a king to be given the great throne of David His ancestor. All the promises of a coming king in the line of David were to be fulfilled in Mary's son. And as the promises made clear, so Gabriel's announcement underlined: His reign would never end. This was the forever king in the line of David (2 Sam. 7), the king anticipated in the great Immanuel account of Isaiah 7-9, born of a virgin, born to reign. Surely this was more than just another great boy child. This was the boy child anticipated through the millennia!

But Mary had a question. She wanted to know how it would happen, given her unmarried virgin status. It is already clear that questioning Gabriel is a dangerous business. But Mary's question is neither rebuked nor disciplined. It is graciously answered. Why? The best explanation seems to lie in her being affirmed for her belief throughout the passage, whereas Zechariah's question communicated a lack of belief. 'Prove it!?' challenged the doubting priest. But Mary's tone was acceptance with legitimate query.

The answer was awesome: the Holy Spirit coming upon her, the power of the Most High overshadowing her, making the child truly God's Son. Gabriel threw in the information about her relative, Elizabeth, and then underlined his point – nothing is impossible with God! Mary's response was surely a delight to the Lord as it was to Gabriel, 'I am the servant of the Lord; let it be to me according to your word' (v. 38).

The thoughts that must have raced through her mind: how will I explain this to my parents, they will be devastated; what will my friends and neighbours think?; and what about poor Joseph? The questions must have swirled, but the posture of her soul was beautiful – I am God's servant, so I trust Him. A lesson to us all in the complexities of life!

Still, she must have longed for someone to talk to about all this. She couldn't go to her parents – they would be heartbroken. And confiding in any friend would make 'virgin' Mary the talk of the lewd grapevine throughout the town. And how could she explain it to Joseph? But Gabriel had offered her a human companion – her relative Elizabeth!

'The wedding is coming soon and this may be my last chance to visit my favourite older cousin (maybe news had spread about Elizabeth's pregnancy), and everyone knows she will be needing help, and...' and somehow the hasty explanation was accepted and Mary travelled south to meet with her cousin.

Elizabeth had suffered decades of social grief over her lack of children. Now in a miracle she was pregnant and after six months it was evident to all. If ever there was a woman ready to talk about her pregnancy it was Elizabeth. Instead, Luke describes her total focus on Mary's faith and Mary's son. Even John celebrated the presence of the Lord in Mary's womb! Months of reading notes from Zechariah and checking the scrolls he pointed to meant that Elizabeth was clear – this was the mother of her Lord!

Furthermore, Mary's fragile faith was affirmed by the elderly saint: Mary was blessed for believing the message of Gabriel (and Elizabeth knew all too well what the alternative looked like!).

MARY'S MAGNIFYING SONG

Perhaps in the midst of the swirling thoughts, the wide-eyed prayers and the longing for someone to understand as she travelled south, Mary had composed a song. Or perhaps it came flooding out in this moment of the relief of being understood and affirmed. Either way, Mary's song truly magnified the Lord.

The song centred on two great themes – God's greatness and her lack of it. Specifically, how her powerful God cares for the weak and the humble. He is a God to rejoice in, for He stoops down to look on the weakest of people. Her privilege was great beyond words, but her being called blessed would be on account of God's goodness to her, not her inherent perfection. It was God's might in action!

What Mary was experiencing first hand was the faithfulness of her great God. His mercy extends from generation to generation. He is a God who makes promises to act and He keeps those promises. His strength had been shown in the scattering of the proud and the humbling of the mighty. At the same time, His strong arm exalted those of humble estate. Perhaps Mary could have been thinking of the muscly arm with clenched fist of judgment and recompense in Isaiah 40:10, the same arm which could tenderly care for the fragile ewe with her young, ever hungry and dependent, holding them close to His heart in verse 11.

As she brought her song to a close, she panned out to show that this faithfulness to multiple generations was truly age-long. God's kindness was not to her alone, but to the nation of which she was an insignificant part. Israel were the seed of Abraham, and that great Seed promised to Abraham had finally come two millennia later. God is powerful and fully able to destroy the proud. But Mary was overwhelmed by how His greatness could be shown in His looking, giving, exalting, feeding and helping in His faithful mercy to His own.

Mary was not a great person, but her faith has been a great example to many through the years. Mary herself was not great, but her child was great. This was the mighty Lord of glory stooping down and stepping into the humble world of a weak humanity. God's strength. Human frailty. Mary's womb.

And they made signs to his father, inquiring what he wanted him to be called. And he asked for a writing tablet and wrote, 'His name is John.' And they all wondered. And immediately his mouth was opened and his tongue loosed, and he spoke, blessing God.
- Luke 1:62-64 -

Hail the heav'n-born Prince of Peace!
Hail the Son of Righteousness!
Light and life to all He brings
Ris'n with healing in His wings[1]

- Charles Wesley, 'Hark the Herald Angels Sing' -

---

1.   Charles Wesley, 'Hark the Herald Angels Sing.' 1739.

16

Say What? Be What?

Luke 1:57-80

For nine months Zechariah had alternated between watching his wife's bump grow bigger, reading and re-reading the scrolls on his table and staring off into space. Oh, and perhaps building a cot for his son and whatever other preparations were done in those days. But he had not been able to say a word.

Finally Elizabeth gave birth to their boy. The whole region was all of a twitter about the amazing news, and many of these neighbours and relatives descended on the house to rejoice with her at God's great mercy. The celebration continued and when the eighth day arrived it was time to circumcise the child. The gathered throng of carers turned the circumcision into a naming ceremony and, like loved ones down through the ages, they had plenty of opinions on what to call the child.

Typically they would expect Grandpa's name to be passed on. Not this time. Perhaps because Grandpa had, himself, passed on many years ago. Or perhaps because Zechariah looked old enough to be the Grandpa, they thought the naming was a foregone conclusion. Surely the boy would take on the name of his father – a godly man and a faithful priest, what greater legacy marker than that?

Elizabeth corrected them all. 'He will be called John.' Opinions don't stop just because the mother reveals a name choice, so they questioned her. After all, they had no relative by the very appropriate God-given name, meaning, well, 'God-given'. So finally the new dad was brought into the conversation by means of awkward signals. (Incidentally, was there any indication that he was deaf during this time?)

Zechariah differed from his wife. He didn't communicate a possible name choice. He was more certain. He had had nine months to ponder things and he knew that if one thing were certain, he would not be uncertain about God's plan in reference to his very special little boy. 'John is his name (already)!' And with that declaration of his faith, Zechariah's trial by silence was brought to an end. His tongue loosed, he began to bless God.

The natural question is this; after all that time, what did he say?

The gathered crowds grew quiet as the presence of divine activity moved them from euphoria and celebration to sober fear. God was at work here. Word spread, and the whole region was talking about the miracle boy of Zechariah.

Their question was natural too: what will this child grow up to be? After all, God was involved, so it must be something special.

The answer to the first question (say what?) also clarifies the second (be what?). What Zechariah finally spoke clarified just who this special boy was to be. He was filled with the Spirit and his torrent of words combined praise with prophecy. After nine months of pondering everything, with Malachi's scroll lying open on the table, Zechariah definitely had something to say!

ZECHARIAH'S PRAISE: GOD IS A FAITHFUL PROMISE KEEPER, A LOVING RESCUER, WHO TRANSFORMS THOSE HE SAVES!
Zechariah is convinced that God is a God who makes promises, and keeps them. Well of course – he lived in Bible times, they all thought that way, didn't they? Hang on a second. Zechariah was toward the end of a long life during which he had seen nothing happening from heaven. No angels, no prophecies, no miracles, nothing. Nor had his parents or grandparents seen anything like that. It was four centuries since the last of the Old Testament prophets had spoken. He lived in a day much like our own. It would be easy to think that if God ever did such things, the time for that is now past. Either God is not able to do such things any more, or maybe God doesn't care.

Zechariah strongly disagrees. He refers to God's promise to David in verse 69, to give him a son to sit on his throne. That was a thousand years before. He mentions the prophets of long ago, in verse 70. Isaiah and Micah both predicted that the descendent of David would sit on his throne and bring peace to the earth, but that was over seven hundred years before. In verses 72-73 he refers to 'our fathers' – the Patriarchs going back to Abraham. God remembered His holy covenant that was made with Abraham. That was almost two thousand years before Zechariah's day! God made promises and then followed decades, centuries, without hint of fulfilment. But Zechariah wanted to shout to the world that God makes promises and He keeps them! He is faithful and He follows through.

Zechariah is thrilled that God loves people, and rescues them. In his song Zechariah refers to God's work of redeeming His people (v. 68), His salvation (v. 69), His work of saving His people from their enemies (v. 71), and His work of deliverance from those enemies (v. 74). That is the kind of God Zechariah is so excited about.

If our problem is so serious that we cannot get out of it ourselves, then we need a rescuer from the outside. Take redemption, for instance. You could go to a slave market and buy back a person from their slavery. The slave was captive and helpless. But you could pay the price and set them free! That was what God was coming to do. That is the kind of God Zechariah knows and celebrates. God came to rescue us not only from our enemies, but from the greatest enemy: sin itself.

Zechariah clarifies the response of the rescued – devoted service to the rescuer! Is this a good deal? Set free from slavery to serve another? Actually, it is! This is the wonderful devotion of a captivated heart. Zechariah uses the term for service used of priests serving in the temple rituals. For Zechariah this made complete sense. We have been rescued and set apart from a world of darkness to be light in the Lord. In a world of evil, by God's grace we can be holy. God's work of salvation is utterly transformative, from the heart out.

ZECHARIAH'S PROPHECY

Here he tells everyone what is going to happen. How does God's rescue actually work? What will God actually do?

Zechariah begins with words for his little boy resting in his hands. This little boy is the prophet of the Most High who will go before the Lord. The Lord is coming and John is to be the preparer of the way for Him! Is he to build a road? No, he will educate the people regarding the real issue.

What is wrong with this world? That was the closing question of a newspaper editorial years ago. G.K. Chesterton responded, 'Dear Sir, in answer to your question, what is wrong with this world? I am.' He was so right. We may be quick to blame the extra evil folk on the news. But the problem is me. The problem is the human heart, for it is from there that evil spews.

John was to prepare the people for the coming of the Lord by sensitising them to the real problem. In verse 80 we are given the summary that he grew and the clock ticked by until his time came to preach. Then we know he preached about the problem of sin and called on the people to repent. That was not a message about fixing themselves, but a message to turn their hearts toward the One whom they had long neglected. It was a message of preparation for a coming Person. We too easily turn repentance into some sort of personal commitment to a higher morality pursued in independent strength, but we lose the focus on the Person!

Biblical repentance is not about turning from bad deeds to good deeds. Rather, it is about turning from the death of self-love to the wonderful Other who to know is life itself.

Then in verses 78-79 Zechariah moves beyond his son, John, to the Lord who will follow. The answer to the darkness is the Light that is coming from heaven. The one to be born of Mary, He is the One who is coming. John is not the rescuer. Jesus is the rescuer!

How does Jesus rescue? Luke, like all the Gospels, points beyond Christmas to Easter. The reason Jesus came to the world was to go to the cross. In a world filled with injustice, there must be justice. There is, and it was demonstrated in the loving sacrifice of Jesus at Calvary. For those who refuse His substitutionary sacrifice, judgment still lies in the future. But the emphasis here is on the tender mercy of a God willing to step in and rescue undeserving sinners.

As the song comes to its finale, it is no surprise to find the language of Malachi spilling out. Gabriel had quoted Malachi to Zechariah in the temple. Surely his heart and mind would have pondered that prophet during those months. With the scroll open he would have rested his eyes on the start of that final great section. 'For behold, the day is coming, burning like an oven, when all the arrogant and all evildoers will be stubble. The day that is coming shall set them ablaze, says the LORD of hosts, so that it will leave them neither root nor branch' (Mal. 4:1). This is scary stuff, but don't miss verse 2: 'But for you who fear my name, the sun of righteousness shall rise with healing in its wings. You shall go out leaping like calves from the stall'!

The deepest and darkest blackness is chased away by the rising of the sun. The valley of the shadow of death is banished by the coming sun of righteousness. Light in darkness. Hope in hopelessness. Peace in conflict. Zechariah knew that we have to look to Jesus, the heavenly gift of the sun of righteousness, rising for those who fear the Lord and trust Him!

And Joseph also went up from Galilee, from the town of Nazareth, to Judea, to the city of David, which is called Bethlehem, because he was of the house and lineage of David, to be registered with Mary, his betrothed, who was with child. And while they were there, the time came for her to give birth.

– Luke 2:4-6 –

We believe in one Lord, Jesus Christ, the only Son of God, eternally begotten of the Father, God from God, Light from Light, true God from true God, begotten, not made, of one Being with the Father. Through him all things were made. For us and for our salvation he came down from heaven: by the power of the Holy Spirit he became incarnate from the Virgin Mary, and was made man. For our sake he was crucified under Pontius Pilate; he suffered death and was buried. On the third day he rose again in accordance with the Scriptures; he ascended into heaven and is seated at the right hand of the Father. He will come again in glory to judge the living and the dead, and his kingdom will have no end.

– The Nicene Creed –

When I am told that God became man, I can follow the idea, but I just do not understand what it means. For what man, if left to his natural promptings, if he were God, would humble himself to lie in the feedbox of a donkey or to hang upon a cross?[1]

– Martin Luther –

---

1. Martin Luther, quoted in Roland Bainton, *Here I Stand: A Life of Martin Luther* (New York: Abingdon Cokesbury, 1950), p. 223.

17

The Birth of the Baby

Luke 2:1-20

The birth of Christ stirs iconic images in our minds. There is the Christmas card image with the snowcapped stable on a Bethlehem hill. Or if you watch most of the Christmas film depictions, you will probably bring to mind Mary on the donkey transitioning into hard labour as they pass the 'Welcome to Bethlehem' sign with night drawing in. Then there is Joseph's frantic pounding on doors, the gruff motel manager peeking around the door with its 'No Vacancies' sign clearly displayed, and the intense thirty seconds of delivery followed by the clean baby boy being held closely by now recovering mother.

You don't have to have experienced a birthing suite to know there are aspects of the standard presentation that fall short of reality! But here is the problem. The iconic nature of the story of that wonderful night can make it seem less than real, somewhere between quaint historical fiction and unbelievable ancient myth. Is the Christmas story just a religious fairy tale? By no means! Luke has gone out of his way, from the beginning of his Gospel, to underline the historicity of what he records. Perhaps we need to hold the iconic images with a very loose grip, while looking carefully to see what is actually stated!

Luke launches into the account with two historical markers. First, the decree of Caesar Augustus for all people to get registered. Second, the identification of which decree this was by his reference to Quirinius' governership of Syria. These are facts, and so is the account that follows.

BIRTH TIME

Joseph has to return to his ancestral hometown of Bethlehem due to the census. Mary is with him, and, importantly, with child. Let's look at verse 6 carefully. 'While they were there, the time came for her to give birth.' That does not feel like a panic-filled arrival, does it? They were there and perhaps they ended up staying longer than expected. Perhaps they knew the journey home to Nazareth would be too risky with her delivery getting closer, so they chose to stay and give birth in Bethlehem. Whatever the circumstances, the account does not sound like a panic-filled, door-pounding, desperation arrival.

Furthermore, in verse 7 we are told that the reason for placing the baby in a manger was that there was no room in the inn. The indications suggest that this was not an ancient Israeli motel chain at all. Bethlehem was a little village on the way to nowhere in particular, so it was unlikely to have a traveller's inn.

There was a term for such a place, and Luke uses it in chapter 10 as he recounts the parable of the Good Samaritan. But that is not the term he uses here in chapter 2. The term he uses here is that which was used for a guest room.

So what Luke seems to be describing is that Joseph and Mary were hosted, probably by a relative, in the house. Not in the guest room, the annexed room typically added on to simple homes, for that was already taken. But what clue do we have that they were in the house? Verse 7 tells us that the baby was laid in a manger. Voila! We all have a manger in our living room, don't we? Well actually, we may be the unusual ones. For three thousand years in the Middle East, single-room homes would have mangers either cut into the floor, or freestanding, because their few animals would be brought in at night. It would not make sense to leave the cow and pair of sheep in a hillside stable just outside the village (not unless they wanted their sustenance to be stolen in the night). No, the animals would be brought inside, the doors bolted and all would be well: animals are safe, and the home has a nighttime heat source!

So perhaps Joseph, the men and the animals were shunted outside as the women of the village helped young Mary give birth to her precious baby. We do a disservice to the people of the Middle East if we think they would fail to help a needy young lady like Mary: we might be uncaring in our culture, but they would not be. A Middle-Eastern village would have taken care of a pregnant total stranger, and certainly would have cared for a member of the extended local family!

The boy who was great, was born in the most humble of circumstances. In fact, he was probably born in a poor family's living room. He came to people like us so that people like us can come to God.

THE SHEPHERDS

Immediately Luke shifts his focus to the lowest of the common folk, a group of shepherds out in the field. An angel came to the shepherds with a good message of great joy for all people, even common shepherds! And what was the news? A baby had been born, a baby given three titles in verse 11 alone.

First, this baby was a Saviour. Ever since the very beginning of history the Jewish people had been waiting for a Saviour, a deliverer, a rescuer coming to set them free.

Second, He is the Messiah, the Christ. This is the anointed One, the special One, the One of God's choosing to do God's work of revealing, representing, ruling.

Third, He is the Lord. He is the One that is in charge of all. You might say the King of Kings and Lord of Lords! And the angel told them that He had been born that very day.

What would you say if you were a shepherd in that group? You might want to check your flask and make sure nobody had tampered with your soup. But they all saw the angel and heard the same message. Strangely, a couple of verses later this group of shepherds rushes off into town to go and see what is happening. That is bizarre, for shepherds would typically stay put. And what is more bizarre is that typical shepherds would not rush off to go and visit royalty!

An angel from heaven announcing the birth of the Saviour, the Messiah, the Lord: not a normal night in the Judean hills. Clearly verse 12 is significant here. The angel gives them a sign. Perhaps the angel's sign was not a treasure hunt clue – that is, let me help you identify the newly born boy-child among the many new babies in the village of Bethlehem. Perhaps the angel's sign stirred the shepherds to go into the town in the first place. How? This royal and unique baby is wrapped in cloths and lying in a manger.

Maybe the angel's sign was like saying to those shepherds, 'go on, you can go visit him, for he isn't in a palace, he's in a manger…you know, the kind of place where you live, the kind of place you'd put your own baby in your house.' Maybe their hearts and minds were stirred by the fact that He came to people like us, so that people like us can come to Him!

That is the point of Christmas – God coming to and becoming like one of us, so that people like us can come to Him.

THE ANGELIC CHORUS

But there was more to the message for the angels. After the birth announcement came the multitude praising God. They said something about heaven and something about earth, something about God and something about humanity.

First of all, the highest of the high, on the throne of the cosmos, God is there; He is on His throne.

But secondly, something has happened on earth. Peace among those with whom God is pleased! The experience of peace is one of the greatest feelings on earth. Conflict over and right relationships restored. It could be hostility between nations, or it could be conflict in the home, but peace is priceless.

Now the holy and just God who sits on the throne of the cosmos would show favour toward people like us?

Wow! That is exactly what the birth of Christ screams for us to hear. God coming to people like us. God stepping in and being born in the most humble of circumstances, a terraced council house in Bethlehem. Just really normal circumstances. Because if He will come near to people like us...

Notice that once the shepherds leave, verse 17, they tell what they have been told. They spread the word, and the word continues to spread around the world. God has not remained distant, but He has stepped into our world. He has come to rescue little nobodies, people without all the right answers, people who are seen by the world as insignificant and people who see themselves as dirty before a holy God.

EASTER ANTICIPATED

The word for a guest room is used again later in the Gospel. In chapter 22 Jesus is in Jerusalem and He sends two disciples ahead of Him to ask a man for the guest room. That was where they were to borrow a room and share the Passover together. What we call the upper room was a guest room (22:11-12). There Jesus co-opts the Passover meal to underline the significance of His being in Jerusalem on this occasion. As he had told them numerous times, He must come to Jerusalem to suffer and die the most ignominious death.

On that night, in that guest room, he explains with the bread that His body was being given for them. He uses the wine to explain that His blood would be poured out for them and initiate the New Covenant. Within 24 hours the symbolism becomes reality and they are stunned at all that took place. But it made sense.

He was born in the most humble of circumstances, so He could die in the most humiliating of circumstances, so that He could make peace between people like us and the kind of God that would do that for us.

At Christmas God came close to us so that we could come close to him. Easter explains how it is possible for people like us to come close to a holy and perfect God.

Life does not work without something else. We are searching for something in a hopeless world and Jesus offers hope. We are searching for something in a conflicted world, maybe in a conflicted life, and Jesus offers peace. We are struggling with bodies that are dying in a world surrounded by death, and Jesus offers us life. And that is the story of Christmas. God coming to people like us, so that people like us can come to Him.

God wants all people to know life. Rich and poor, male and female, all people. God came and gave His life to make ours possible.

'Lord, now you are letting your servant depart in peace, according to your word; for my eyes have seen your salvation that you have prepared in the presence of all peoples, a light for revelation to the Gentiles, and for glory to your people Israel.'
– Luke 2:29-32 –

Did you know, that your baby boy has walked where angels trod?
When you kiss your little baby, you've kissed the face of God.
Mary, did you know that your baby boy is Lord of all creation?
Mary, did you know that your baby boy will one day rule the nations?
Did you know, that your baby boy is heaven's perfect lamb?
This sleeping child you're holding, is the great I AM![1]

– Mark Lowry, 'Mary Did You Know?' –

1.   Mark Lowry, 'Mary Did You Know?' 1984.

18

Awaiting the Person of Peace

Luke 2:21-40

Peace. It is a word often associated with Christmas. Tranquil, snowy scenes are finished off with references to 'Peace on Earth'. Famously, during the First World War soldiers got out of trenches on both sides and played a game of football together in no-man's-land. Was this simply an innate sense of nostalgia and memories of peaceful Christmas times with families, loved ones and comforting traditions? It may have been that for some, but there is a stronger connection here.

For many of us, Christmas season is a time of busy and frantic preparations, shopping, wrapping, cooking, travelling, socialising, etc. Then with the soporific effect of turkey comes a couple of hours of tranquility and peace, before nerves get frayed and the peace disperses like a mist. But that is not the peace of Christmas.

THE PEACE OF CHRISTMAS

All through Luke's infancy account we find hints and references to peace. Zechariah was told that his special boy would restore relationships both horizontally and vertically in anticipation of the Lord's coming. Mary was told that her greater special boy would sit on the throne of His father David, reigning forever, a kingdom without end. This is that kingdom and reign described in Isaiah 9 as belonging to the Prince of Peace, whose government *and peace* would be unending. Zechariah sang of the coming of the manifestation of God's tender mercy who will guide our feet into the path of peace. And then, the shepherds were also told of the Davidic king, experiencing the thrilling crescendo from the heavens: 'Glory to God in the highest, and on earth, peace to men on whom God's favour rests!'

Peace is like a dominant thread woven throughout the account, and sure enough, it resurfaces one more time before the section is over. After the amazed shepherds leave, we read of Jesus being circumcised and named with the name given by the angel. Then comes verse 22. This seems to imply the passing of a few weeks. Perhaps the hasty departure within a night or two of the hasty arrival needs revisiting.

A few weeks after the birth, Mary and Joseph head up to Jerusalem and into the temple courts. Luke's account began in the temple, and he brings the infancy account full circle with the greater boy and favoured parent heading into the place where Zechariah had stumbled out speechless but bursting just over a year before.

Mary and Joseph had some ritual uncleanness issues to take care of after the birth. They also wanted to redeem this firstborn son with the obligatory offering (they choose the lower cost option, reflecting their financial status). Furthermore, they may well be bringing Jesus with them in an act of dedicating Him, somewhat like Hannah with Samuel. So with all this in mind, this young and very insignificant couple head into the temple courts.

Young couples with their first child are so careful (older couples with their fourth or fifth tend to be a bit bolder in the way they swing the carseat around!). It is easy to imagine young teen Mary carrying her precious bundle so carefully. And Joseph, her devoted husband-to-be, fulfilling the protector's role as he made sure she was able to take each step. 'Excuse us! Pardon me! Thank you.' Just another couple, with just another baby. But they weren't just another couple. And He certainly wasn't just another baby. God wanted the world to know who this baby was!

So God placed a pair of people in the temple to meet the young family. Luke is piling on the pairs: two angelic announcements, two songs of celebration, two special boys born, and now, two special witnesses. Simeon and Anna. Male and female. Luke enjoys pairing male and female characters in his Gospel. A couple of dozen pairs can be found with both a man and woman included. This Jesus is for everyone – poor folk like shepherds, and for both men and women too.

WITNESS 1: SIMEON

Simeon was righteous and devout, and he was waiting for the consolation of Israel. That is, he was waiting for God to make things right with His covenant people. What's more,

Luke tells us that the Holy Spirit was upon him and he had been informed that he would not die until he had seen the Messiah, the Lord's Christ.

Here was one man that was not going to step aside for protector Joseph. Simeon would have pondered many times God's promise of the coming of the deliverer to Adam and Eve, God's promised seed of blessing to Abram, God's promised coming King in the line of David. And now, perhaps hardly able to take a full breath he was so excited, he moves into the temple to rendez-vous with an unsuspecting young couple.

So Simeon took Jesus in his arms and praised God! It is hard to imagine that Mary would have given over her baby boy to a stranger very easily, but this elderly man obviously posed no threat.

WITNESS 2: ANNA

Before looking at Simeon's words, scan down to verse 36 and meet the second witness – an even more remarkable individual. Elderly Anna was living in the temple courts. Incidentally, add the Hebrew 'h' at the start of her name and don't miss the déjà-vu here: Hannah in the house of God for the dedication of a precious baby boy!

Elderly may be an understatement. Anna had either been a widow from about twenty to her mid-eighties, or possibly, she had been a widow for eighty-four years. (That would mean she was now over a century old!) She never left the temple; obviously special arrangements had been made for a senior saint! She was a worshipper, a prayer warrior. And now she adds her words to Simeon, proclaiming gratitude to God and speaking to all who were waiting for the redemption of Jerusalem.

In an oral and religious culture this pair of precious saints function like great heavenly highlighter pens making sure that everyone knows just how special this little boy really is!

SIMEON'S SPEECH

So what was it that Simeon actually said? Back to verse 29. Five quick points to note.

1. This baby boy is God's salvation. All those centuries of longing and waiting and praying and begging God, 'would you do something, save us Lord!' Here He is. Six, seven, eight pounds of baby boy. And He is God's salvation.

The root cause of all the conflict in the world and in our homes and in ourselves, the root of it is our fist-shaking at heaven. Some express their rebellion in gross evil, but others shake their fists at God by being very self-righteous and upright in the world's eyes, by trying to be as good as the next person and better than the criminal sinners we see on TV. But this independence is still rebellion. And God has wrapped up His whole salvation plan in that little baby boy.

2. Jesus is for all people. In verse 32 he refers to the Gentiles and Israel. That covers everyone. There is Israel, and there is everyone else: all nations. Jesus is the only option. Not just locally, but for all of us.

3. Jesus will be massively controversial. See what he says in verse 34: rising and falling, a sign opposed, hearts revealed. Even today, if you talk about God in a conversation, you won't get much reaction. If you pray in a public event, just pray to God and you will be fine. But bring Jesus into the mix and suddenly things tend to get divided. Jesus polarises people.

A generic God feels safe and distant. But when we talk about Jesus we are talking about God stepping in and getting too close for comfort. Notice how John 3:16 is followed by two verses that speak of how people are condemned because of not believing in Jesus. Nobody will ever stand before God and having rejected Jesus still have a plea to make to God. Notice the final verses of John 3. The Father's love for the Son is the source of the issue. Either we love the Son like the Father does or we reject Him.

The exclusivity of Jesus is uncomfortable. Jesus is controversial.

4. Jesus will be painful for Mary. I wonder how many nights Mary lay awake pondering how and when a sword would pierce her soul because of this child? We don't know what happened to Joseph, but Mary was still around when Jesus embarked on His ministry. She was there when Jesus and His disciples arrived at the wedding in Cana. She was there when Jesus was working miracles, she was there when He became popular. She was there when He became more controversial. She was there that first Easter when He was led out to be crucified. Nailed to the wood and elevated in the most agonising death the Romans could devise or perfect, and Mary was right there.

5. Simeon was ready to be dismissed in peace. Notice verse 29. This speech is known in some churches as the *Nunc Dimittis* (Now dismiss me). An amazing thought to centre our hearts on at the climax of Luke's infancy narrative.

NUNC DIMITTIS
Simeon has been told he would see the Christ. He's looking into the eyes of this little boy, and now he knows there is

nothing left to see or do. He's happy and ready to go home to heaven. If I die now, I die in peace. A specific reality for Simeon.

But if we pan out from that moment, we have the same issue. With looming judgment hanging over us we live in fear of death. For the past two thousand years Jesus has been preached around the world. And for the past two thousand years people have discovered that once they catch a glimpse of Jesus, God's salvation, then death is not the great enemy anymore. The world has been overrun by an army of Simeons: having seen Jesus, they are ready to die. Ready to be martyred. Ready to step into eternity.

After pondering Luke's account of the birth of the Saviour, are we convinced? Has he piled up enough pairs of witnesses to make a Simeon of us? By the way, he adds a second temple visit for Jesus. It is the only glimpse we have of Jesus between infancy and adulthood. Again, in the temple, a pair of people are looking for Him. Again, His greatness and uniqueness are declared in the temple courts.

So where does this leave us? Having seen Jesus, I have seen God's salvation and now not even death threatens me. Christmas is not about two hours of turkey-induced peace. Christmas peace is not merely momentary tranquility. Instead, Christmas is about peace with our Creator so that we can enjoy life to the full, a relationship with Him, and a peace that leaves us ready to go home whenever God should call.

PART FOUR:

Cur Deus Homo – Why Did God Become Man?

New Testament Reflections

But when the fullness of time had come, God sent forth his Son, born of woman, born under the law, to redeem those who were under the law, so that we might receive adoption as sons. And because you are sons, God has sent the Spirit of his Son into our hearts, crying, 'Abba! Father!'
- Galatians 4:4-6 -

Whenever you are concerned to think and act about your salvation, you must put away all speculations about the Majesty, all thoughts of works, traditions, and philosophy – indeed, of the Law of God itself. And you must run directly to the manger and the mother's womb, embrace this Infant and Virgin's Child in your arms, and look at Him – born, being nursed, growing up, going about in human society, teaching, dying, rising again, ascending above all the heavens, and having authority over all things. In this way you can shake off all terrors and errors, as the sun dispels the clouds.[1]

- Martin Luther, *Lectures on Galatians* -

---

1. Martin Luther, *Lectures on Galatians*, 1535 edition in *Luther's Works,* vol.26 (Concordia, 1963), p. 30.

19

Galatians: Perfect Timing!

The first of Paul's letters was written after the first of Paul's journeys. He had preached the gospel of grace and seen churches planted as people trusted in Christ, the man of God's great promise. But soon after he moved on, false teachers moved in.

Paul, they said, was not a real apostle, but a junior figure compared to the big guns in Jerusalem. And his grace gospel was only half a message, it was imbalanced. If the Galatians wanted to be fully born again, and not just born a bit, then they needed to observe the Law, with circumcision as a focal point. And if they wanted to live lives that truly pleased God then they needed to observe the Law. Grace and Law was the real deal.

Paul got wind of this and immediately wrote his stinging letter to the Galatians. He defended his apostleship and his gospel. He was not subordinate to the Jerusalem apostles, in fact they affirmed his message and he even opposed Peter when he had compromised one time. And his message was not imbalanced. To try to add Law to Grace was actually to turn away from God! (See 1:6)

By the end of chapter 2 and the start of 3, Paul is really driving home his main point. We are justified by faith in Jesus Christ, not by works of the Law. Consequently, once saved, we continue to live by faith. But someone seemed to have cast a spell on the Galatians. Paul had preached in such a way as to effectively paste up a billboard of Christ crucified before them. In faith they had trusted in Him to receive the gift of the promise, who is the Spirit. But now they had fallen for the idea of maturing and growing by the efforts of their flesh!

THE GOSPEL AND THE PROMISE

So Paul looked back to the promise God made to Abraham, identifying faith as the key to salvation, and calling it the gospel (3:8). The great blessing that was to come through Abraham to the Gentiles was, in fact, the promised Spirit (3:14). So the focus of the seed promise was not multiple, but singular: Christ (3:16).

God's promise came centuries before the Law, so the great inheritance offered could not depend on the Law, but on God's promise (3:18). The Law was not opposed to God's promises, but neither was it intended to solve the sin problem. Rather, it was added to guard and guide sinners until the Promised One should come, and then all could put their faith in Him and become part of Abraham's seed (3:29).

The Law is like the rumble strips beside the motorway. They are good and they serve a good purpose, but they don't make you a good driver. You certainly wouldn't want to be a passenger with a driver who constantly edged on to the rumble strips in order to know where to go. The Law warns us when we are going out of bounds, but it doesn't help us positively discover righteousness (for example, simply avoiding adultery doesn't make you a good spouse).

In fact, the tendency of the flesh in a post-Genesis 3 world is to abuse the Law by curving back in on ourselves. We look at the code, but instead of comparing ourselves to it and finding ourselves wanting, we selectively compare ourselves to others and suddenly we are doing alright! Paul knew the fruit of this new theology would result in competitiveness and a loss of love for one another, so he addressed that in chapter 5.

The solution to the sin problem has never been the Law. From the very beginning the need has been for faith – trusting in God's word, in His promise, in Him. In fact, Paul points to Christ, the person of the Promise, and to the Spirit as the solution to sin. This is true both for initial justification and for living out a God-pleasing life. To turn from this New Covenant package back to some version of the Old Covenant is to turn from faith to effort, from God to self.

DIVINE PLAN, PERFECT TIMING

At the start of chapter 4 Paul is describing the immature state of God's people under the guardianship of the Law. 'But when the fullness of time had come, God sent forth his Son, born of a woman, born under the law, to redeem those who were under the law, so that we might receive adoption as sons' (vv. 4-5).

Jesus came at just the right time. Some look to understand the timing in terms of the political and societal situation, with the Roman road system in place, the Greek language spread across the empire, the Jewish hopes and religious anticipations bubbling yet the nation in desperate need. Indeed, it does seem that the timing of Jesus' coming with all the appropriate conditions in place facilitated the spread of the gospel message in that first generation.

But the passage is not pointing to issues of the spreading of the message, it is pointing to the timing of Christ's arrival in respect to the people of Israel. Tying back to the great promise of Genesis 3:15, Paul identifies God's son as one born of a woman. Here is the seed of the woman! He was born under the law, and as a Jew in Israel He became part of that people being held imprisoned by the Law until redemption was possible. And He came to redeem those imprisoned ones, resulting not in further slavery, but in the maturity and freedom of adoption as sons.

Not under the Law, but in Christ. Not a slave, but a son!

Sonship by the Restored Spirit

Paul goes on in 4:6 to identify the great benefit of being adopted as sons—the presence of the Spirit of God! Back in Eden the Spirit was lost, the One who bonds Father and Son within the Trinity, and who was the loving bond between Adam and Eve, and between them and God. But now, finally, in the fullness of time, the Spirit is again fully restored to the hearts of God's people. What is the result? Notice it is not an immediate emphasis on empowerment or behaviour (our post-fall tendency is to want whatever we need to be able to perform independently, which is why our thoughts move in that direction). No, Paul points to the presence of the Spirit as the bond of love that cries out within us, 'Abba! Father!'

This is the cry of intimacy and unity with God Himself. This is the cry of a totally dependent child who fully trusts in their Daddy because if I am with him then all is well!

The gospel was never about striving in our own efforts to keep the Law and live good independent lives. The gospel was always about trusting in God's promise and God's presence.

This is why Paul was so flummoxed by the Galatians. Why were they turning away from God? He returns to Abraham and draws out an analogy concerning the son from the free woman and the son from the slave. The one represents the goodness of God's good news and plan that is associated with the 'Jerusalem above'. The other represents the enslavement associated with Mt Sinai and the present earthly, Law-bound Jerusalem. He is urging them to trust in the promise and the presence, the Son and the Spirit, the new covenant and not the old.

APPLYING THE PROMISE GOSPEL

In the last two chapters Paul summarises and applies what he has presented. The summary is repeated as a pair of thoughts. In 5:5-6 he points to the Spirit and to faith in Christ, which is worked out not in the Law, but in love. In 6:14-15 he summarises his message again, this time pointing to the cross of Christ, dismissing issues of circumcision, but affirming that it is only the new creation that counts for anything. What is the new creation? He later develops that thought further in 2 Corinthians 1-5, another great New Covenant passage. So he is again pointing to both Christ (directly) and the Spirit (indirectly). In fact, even in his final verse he subtly reinforces the pairing again: the grace of our Lord Jesus Christ be with your spirit (6:18). This is not the capital 'S' Holy Spirit, or is it? If they have any spirit, in light of all that has gone before, perhaps it is only due to the presence of God's Spirit.

And what is the application? Paul offers that in terms of freedom, faith and fruit. The enslavement of the Law is over, but this doesn't mean Christians are free to serve their own flesh. Rather they are free to serve one another in love (5:13). Before sin entered in Genesis 3, the freedom of the Spirit meant the freedom to serve and to love. Now in the New Covenant there is an expectation of the same.

Paul calls them to faith in Christ, walking in step with the Spirit who is within, a Spirit whose delight is toward Abba and toward others. And the fruit that comes from living by the Spirit is first and foremost love, a love that manifests in joy and peace, patience and kindness, goodness and faithfulness, gentleness and self-control.

Paul's gospel was critiqued for being light on sin. Actually he turned the critique right around. It is only in the gospel of grace that we can live lives marked by selflessness and love, doing good to everyone. This gospel of grace means looking to the Promised One and living by the presence of the Spirit who bonds us to God and each other. When we turn back to ourselves, even if under the guise of seeking to please God through keeping laws, then the fruit of the flesh turns out to be very negative—loss of love (4:15), biting and devouring one another (5:15), arrogance and competition (5:26), as well as the whole list of the works of the flesh (5:19-21—incidentally, why do we only ever associate this list with the world beyond the church? The whole context is pointing to this list as the ultimate destination of the trajectory of fleshly religiosity).

Faith Problem, Faith Solution

Galatians is not the easiest letter to grasp, but its message is life-changing. The gospel which God promised way back in Abraham's day is the only solution to the problem caused even earlier—in the Garden of Eden. The problem was a faith problem. The solution is a faith solution. The solution has never been about striving, effort, works, flesh and religiousness. The solution has never been a what-to-do, but always a who-to-trust.

So look to the Promised One, Jesus, who was crucified to deal with sin and draw us out of our self-obsession and into relationship with God. Lean on the Spirit, whose restoration means life since life is found in the delightful bond of relationship with God our Abba! Live out this love toward God and toward neighbour, and we will be closer to God's original and ultimate plan than ever before.

*For the grace of God has appeared, bringing salvation
for all people, training us to renounce ungodliness and
worldly passions, and to live self-controlled, upright,
and godly lives in the present age, waiting for our
blessed hope, the appearing of the glory of our great
God and Saviour Jesus Christ, who gave himself for
us to redeem us from all lawlessness and to purify
for himself a people for his own possession who are
zealous for good works.*
- Titus 2:11-14 -

*What He was He continued to be; what He was not
He took to Himself.[1]*
- Gregory of Nazianzus -

*Now He's standing in the place of honour,
Crowned with glory on the highest throne,
Interceding for His own beloved
Till His Father calls us to bring them home!
Then the skies will part, as the trumpet sounds
Hope of heaven or the fear of hell;
But the Bride will run, to her Lover's arms,
Giving glory to Immanuel![2]*
- Stuart Townend, 'Immanuel' -

---

1. Gregory of Nazianzus, *Orations* XXIX.19.
2. Stuart Townend, 'Immanuel', 1999.

20

Titus:
Grace Appeared!

Self-controlled, upright and godly lives. Zealous and eager for good works. How are we supposed to achieve such ideal goals in our moral lives? What is the mechanism for achieving these ideals? Is there anywhere we can go, apart from Galatians, to reinforce the same teaching? Absolutely. There are plenty of options. How about we visit Titus for a few minutes?

Titus is a fantastic little letter. Sadly, it is often treated as a mini-1 Timothy and then essentially overlooked. It was sent from Paul to Titus to help him in his work as Paul's representative on Crete. The church had been planted, but there were still some establishing and leadership issues to be addressed.

46 VERSES OF PRACTICAL IMPACT

Titus is short, just 46 verses in total. Each of the three chapters begin with some practical instruction. Then Paul transitions to an explanation of the underlying truth that drives such instruction.

In the first chapter Paul calls for the appointment of godly elders and lists the appropriate qualifications. Verse 10—'For…' Here is why they needed elders to be recognised and appointed: because of the threats to the church. Paul notes both the state of the Cretan culture and the presence of 'the circumcision' party with their false motives. The church needed elders in place to feed, lead, care and protect the flock.

In the second chapter Paul urges Titus to teach application fitting for sound doctrine. So he goes through instructions for the different groups that comprised the church. Their good belief should be dressed in appropriate applicational garb. Why? Verse 11—'For…' Let's come back to this one, but first spot how chapter 3 follows the same pattern.

In the third chapter Paul wants the believers to be reminded regarding their conduct toward outsiders too. Why? Verse 3—'For…' It was because, prior to salvation, the Christians were also enslaved by their worldly passions, full of hatred and folly. But a transformation occurred. How? By the kindness, love and mercy of God. In saving them, God had poured out the Spirit to add hope to gracious justification. By the giving of the Spirit their worldly passions were captured by a whole new kind of affection, even the expulsive power of a greater affection!

SPOTLIGHT ONE

Coming back to chapter 2, we read Paul's ten verses of targeted applicational content. Then we see the underlying doctrine that would drive such Christian living in the church context. It was all because of salvation. In fact, it was all in response to the first coming of Christ—grace personified!

In these later letters to Timothy and Titus, Paul really picks up his use of the notion of an 'epiphany' – that is, an appearing. It was a term that the Romans were starting to use in respect to the emperor. The concept of emperor-worship was starting to emerge, and to encourage it, the emperors would sometimes go into seclusion for a while. When they finally went public again, they would do so in a spectacular fashion, with all spotlights on them. It was all intended to stir the crowds by the god-like presentation of the great Caesar they were expected to hail.

In the movie *Gladiator* there is a moment that captures this idea. Insecure but self-loving Emperor Commodus, arrayed impressively in white, 'appeared' spectacularly through the floor of the Colosseum. His glorious appearing backfired in the film, but the effect on the crowds of such an entrance would have been powerful.

Paul took the same term and redeemed it, using it appropriately for the appearing of the true God. Once we have eyes to see, we know that Jesus really did pull off a stunning 'entry of a God!' In fact, Paul does not qualify the name of Jesus with the quality of grace, he simply presents him as grace personified. The grace of God has appeared!

LIVES TRANSFORMED

So does Paul then offer a caveat and pull in some external pressure to avoid sin and the abuse of grace? Perhaps he pulls in a reference to the circumcision party and corrects their mishandling of the Law? Not at all. Paul writes that 'it' teaches us. What does? What teaches us? The grace of God teaches us, trains us, changes us. Because of the coming of the grace of God we are changed by new affections expelling old passions. We are changed by the grace of God to live self-controlled, upright and godly lives in the now. Really? Grace does that? That's what Paul says.

He comes back to this transformation in chapter 3, adding the work of the Spirit to the person of Christ but reinforcing the sense that it is God's kindness and grace and mercy that do the work of life transformation.

The grace of God in Christ is certainly a powerful force—imagine what it would take to transform ungodly sinners so that their very passions were no longer worldly. Imagine what it would take to transform sinners into self-controlled, upright and godly folk. Imagine what it would take to stir within a now-obsessed people a future-oriented hope. It would surely take something like God's grace appearing, all dressed up in human flesh.

SPOTLIGHT TWO
It is the grace of God in the first coming of Christ that creates a longing in our hearts for the second coming, His glorious appearing—He who is our great God and Saviour! The great and blessed hope of the Christian is not a package of benefits in heaven, it is Christ Himself.

This great God and Saviour who will come into our world again by the most glorious appearing is the One who came to reveal God's heart to us the first time. It was a heart of grace: a giving, not a grabbing heart. For He gave Himself to buy us back from all wickedness and to purify a people of His own. The people who were once drunk on worldly passions are now transformed morally, for they are pure. And they are transformed affectively, for they are zealous, eager to do what is good.

LIVING IN THE SHADOWS

We live our lives in the shadowlands between two great spotlights. So we look back to God's grace bursting into our self-absorbed world in the form of self-giving grace personified. We look forward to our great God and Saviour appearing gloriously once more. And we live now, washed by the inner renewal of the Spirit Himself. Not looking to ourselves and our effort and our personal drive for pure living. Rather, we live looking toward Christ, grace personified, who shapes us into His very own people, transformed from the inside out.

Christ Jesus, who, though he was in the form of God,
did not count equality with God
a thing to be grasped, but emptied himself,
by taking the form of a servant,
being born in the likeness of men.
And being found in human form,
he humbled himself by becoming obedient
to the point of death, even death on a cross.
– Philippians 2:5-8 –

Man's maker was made man that He, Ruler of the stars,
might nurse at His mother's breast;
that the Bread might hunger, the Fountain thirst,
the Light sleep, the Way be tired on its journey;
that Truth might be accused of false witnesses,
the Teacher be beaten with whips,
the Foundation be suspended on wood;
that Strength might grow weak;
that the Healer might be wounded; that Life might die.[1]
– Augustine of Hippo –

---

1.   St.Augustine, *Sermons* 191.1.

21

Philippians:
God Humbled!

If you pick up a systematic theology textbook you will typically find that the early chapters are concerned with defining God's essence. What is He, really? And typically you will find a list of attributes that seek to do that work of definition. Where these attribute lists come from is not our concern here (although it should be our concern somewhere). Rather than pondering God's omniscience (all-knowing-ness) and omnipresence (everywhere-present-ness), etc., let's ponder an attribute often omitted from these lists. God's humility.

Some years ago I was startled by Psalm 113. It begins in usual fashion urging everyone everywhere to praise the LORD. Why? Because there is nobody else like the LORD our God, enthroned on high, yet who humbles Himself

(vv. 5-6, NASB). Does God really humble himself? Is this just a quaint notion, a poetic description from the Psalmist's creative pen? Not at all; let's head to one of the New Testament's most familiar passages: Philippians chapter 2.

PAUL'S PARTNERSHIP CORRESPONDENCE

Paul was in prison when he wrote Philippians. The church there had shown great care for him, and Paul really cared for them. The result was the favourite letter of many Bible readers today. In the first chapter Paul expresses thanks for them and their partnership with him in the work of the gospel. He describes his situation and the tension he feels between staying and going home to be with the Lord. He concludes the chapter with the big idea for all that will follow: he wants them, in their gospel ministry, to stand firm in the face of opposition, and to stand firm together, united.

So the book then develops these two great thoughts. Unity in chapter two, and then steadfast perseverance in chapter three. The last chapter reviews these two themes in tangible ways and then concludes with more details revealing his connection with the believers in Philippi.

Chapter two is so well known but it is often misconstrued. Here is how not to understand the passage: 'In the first two verses Paul piles on the pressure by essentially stating that if you have received any benefits, then you owe everyone a duty of commitment to church unity. So don't be selfish, but force yourself to look out for the interests of others (vv. 3-4). In fact, Jesus did His duty perfectly, so copy Him (vv. 5-8)' . . . alright, that's enough of that. Let's try again:

Paul launches the chapter with some reflections on the privilege of participation in the divine life – the language of participation in the Spirit, being in Christ, comforted by His love, etc. Then he gets to his instruction, his main idea.

In verses 3-4 he gives the key to being united as believers: the Philippians need to humbly look out for others and not just themselves. Self-focused concern divides, but concern for others is the glue that binds a community together.

Then he reinforces his point with several examples of self-giving: in response to Christ in verses 5-11, in response to Paul's example and teaching in verses 12-18, in response to Timothy's self-giving example in verses 19-24, and finally, in response to Epaphroditus' willingness to give his life in verses 25-30. For our purposes here we need only zero in on the self-giving humility of Christ.

The famous section dealing with Christ's humiliation and exaltation was probably an early hymn already in circulation by the time Paul wrote Philippians. It certainly has the feel of a hymn. The first part is all downwards, the second is all upwards.

Down, But How Low?

In verses 6 to 8 the reader watches the epic journey of the incarnation and the passion of Christ. He was not just born, He already was. Fully God, equally God, there. But He did not cling on to those rights and privileges. Instead He became a man. In the terms of the hymn, and in contrast to what was always true before, this was the equivalent of making Himself nothing! The incarnation is about the Son of God choosing to become nothing – this could have been a compelling title for this book: *Pleased to become as nothing as you!*

Actually, He went farther than that. Even having traversed the great divide between divine and human, heaven and earth, the throne and the manger, the Son went farther still. He humbled Himself and became obedient to the point of death. Obedient to whom? It was the Father's will. And what kind of death? Even death on a cross!

Is it possible to think of a more humiliating and degrading way to die? The Romans had perfected the art of keeping criminals alive as long as possible to serve as the ultimate deterrent for as long as possible. Books like this one don't even describe all the humiliation of crucifixion, because it is so much worse than our sanctified and stained-glass images ever portray. To become a human was incredible, but to go as far as dying on the cross, that should stir a creation-wide gasp. More of that in a minute. The incarnation was not an end in itself, as we so often say at Christmas. The reason for Christmas is Easter; the manger was the direct route to the cross.

UP, BUT HOW FAR?

I remember hearing a preacher describe a hypothetical conversation within the Trinity. Imagine the Father speaking to the Son, *'Son, I am sending you on a mission, I want you to go to the earth, become a man, and show them what I am like.'*

The Son, of course, delights to do the Father's will: *'Father, I would be thrilled to do that, I want them all to know exactly how great and good you are!'*

So the Son came to earth and was born humbly in a peasant's home. He grew up as a humble carpenter's stepson. He performed His ministry, humbly avoiding fame while giving Himself away to His disciples and to the needy folk that crossed His path. And then came the cross, in the terms of John's Gospel, the hour for which He came, the time of His glorification. Having been fully glorified, or should I say, humiliated, He returns after the resurrection to the Father. The conversation continues,

'Son, that was perfect! Now they know exactly what I am like!'

Hold on a minute. Is this accurate? Surely this is Jesus *in His humanity* . . . and surely that is different from the divine version of Jesus? Surely God the Father is entirely different, you know, bright shiny different? Our theology may affirm this thought, but what is the Bible teaching? Back in Exodus was the glory of God all about power, or primarily focused on His goodness and love and mercy? In John's Gospel is not the glorification of Christ and the Father entirely wrapped up in the event of the crucifixion? In fact, what does Jesus say when asked for a glimpse of the Father in John 14? *If you have seen me, you have seen the Father!*

Back to Philippians 2. What is God's response to Jesus' humiliation on the cross? He has highly exalted Him and given Him the name above every name, so that at His name every knee will bow and every tongue confess. (By the way, this is all Isaiah 45:18-23 language. God the LORD is uniquely worthy of praise, and now in Philippians He is pointing all praise to His Son!) So what name does everyone confess? It is that Jesus the Messiah is Lord.

Here we need to go a bit deeper for a couple of lines. The Greek-speaking Jewish background believers could not glibly say that Jesus Christ is Lord. The word Lord presents an issue. After all, in the Hebrew, Jews don't pronounce the name of God, YHWH (typically written Yahweh today). When they see that name they would articulate *Adonai* (Hebrew for Lord). This convention carried over into the Greek translation of the Hebrew Scriptures as they would substitute *Kurios* (Greek for Lord) in place of the name Yahweh. This is why our English Bibles use all capitals for LORD when translating Yahweh. So what? Well, all that to say that Jewish-background believers are not going to glibly refer to Jesus essentially as Yahweh, but that is the climax of this early hymn, and all to the glory of God the Father!

The self-humiliation of the Son was the perfect presentation of the nature of God the Father. Really?

Let's jump to a familiar story of Jesus to reinforce the point. We looked at it briefly earlier.

Two Lost Sons, One Unusual Father

When Jesus was enjoying the company of tax collectors and sinners the religious elite grew grumbly. So He told them a parable. First there was the sheep lost in the far country and found by the shepherd, followed by a party to celebrate. Second there was the coin lost in the home and found by the woman, followed by a party to celebrate. That was all introductory set up, then Jesus got to the fully developed story (see Luke 15:11-32).

There was a man who had two sons. This was not just any man, as it will turn out. This man, the father in the story, is unusual three-times over. For a start, he allows his younger son to spurn his love and wish him dead. A normal Middle-Eastern man with all the pride and dignity that would come from his wealth and standing in the community would not let his son reject him. He would save face and force the issue his way. But not this man. Instead, when his son bizarrely wishes him dead already, he hands over the inheritance and watches the young man lose a fortune in a fire sale, load up his wallet and head for the highway.

Some time later, when that son comes back toward home, stinking of pig and desperately broke, armed with nothing but a job-application speech (for he wanted to get a paid position in his father's business), the father does it again. Not only did he let him go, now he does the unthinkable – he runs! He hoists up his skirts and bares his legs and runs through the town in front of everybody in order to get to his son and rescue him from the hostile local folk. This stunning display of self-humiliation ruins the job-application speech and the son can only gawp at such amazing grace as he is led into the party, dressed in his father's robe, wearing the shoes of privilege and carrying the credit card of its day on one of his fingers!

Lost. Found. Party. Perfect. But Jesus is not finished yet. There is still the older son. He is out and misses the action, returning in time to take his place at the party. Instead he stands outside fuming mad at his father. Just like his brother, he humiliates his father publically. Just like with his brother, the father comes out and humiliates himself in order to rescue him. Imagine the whole village with a drumstick in one hand and a burger in the other, looking out of the window as the father begs his son to come in to the party.

Three times the father does the unthinkable. He lets the son spurn him. Then he humiliates himself to rescue first the younger, then the older brother. Both wanted to be employed by their father, they had no inclination towards relationship. Both wanted the company of others. Both wanted to be paid: the younger son knew the father would pay better than the pig farmer, while the older son had nothing with which to compare his pay but knew that he hadn't received even a goat to party with his friends. Both wanted a contract, but the father wanted relationship. And he knew that there was no way these two hearts would voluntarily turn towards him of their own accord.

He needed to do something to rescue them. So he did. He took the journey to them. He humiliated himself for them. One, like a sheep, was lost in the far country. One, like a coin, was lost in the home. The father did everything to win both back.

So, who is the father? Is this the heart of God demonstrated in story form? Or is this the heart of Christ? The answer is a resounding yes! It is Jesus who goes through the humiliation for our redemption, but in doing so He perfectly reveals the Father to us.

The humility of God is revealed in Christ, who ran humiliated into this world for us!

But we see him who for a little while was made lower than the angels, namely Jesus, crowned with glory and honour because of the suffering of death, so that by the grace of God he might taste death for everyone.
- Hebrews 2:9 -

He is a mediator because he is human and, as a human, shows us that to attain that supreme good, blessed and beatific, we need not seek other mediators to serve like rungs on a ladder of ascent. For the blessed God who makes us blessed by deigning to share our humanity showed us the shortest way to sharing in his divinity. Freeing us from mortality and misery, he leads us, not to the immortal blessed angels so as to become immortal and blessed by sharing in their nature, but to that Trinity in communion with which even the angels are blessed. When, then, in order to be mediator, he willed to take 'the form of a servant' below the angels, he remained in the form of God above the angels, being simultaneously the way of life on earth and life itself in heaven.[1]

- Augustine of Hippo, *City of God* -

22

Hebrews:
Lower than Angels!

It is exciting to read the sermons in the book of Acts: Peter at Pentecost, Stephen before the Sanhedrin, Paul on trial. But these are really 'just' inspired summaries. What would we give for a full sermon manuscript from the era of the apostles? Actually, we have one, and what a sermon it is – the 'book' of Hebrews.

In the PS added at the end, the writer refers to the book as a 'word of exhortation' – the same label used in Acts 13:15 to refer to a spoken message in a synagogue. Throughout the letter Hebrews does not act like a letter. All the conventions for letter writing are ignored, but all the traits of a preached message are present: references to speaking, hearing and listening; transition sections between main points; direct exhortation; and even slight verbal imprecision (i.e. Heb. 2:6; 4:4).

This sermon has an introduction followed by the main idea from a single Old Testament passage. That main idea is then developed in three movements, each explaining and applying another Old Testament passage. There are clear transitions between each section and the conclusion drives home the whole message in a final salvo of exhortation. It is a masterful piece of sermonic brilliance.

Let's walk through the sermon briefly, noting the significance of the incarnation as we go.[1]

INTRODUCTION: A SON SUPERSEDES ANY ANGEL (1:1-14)

God has always been communicating Himself to people, but the ultimate communication is through His Son. So the preacher launches with a spectacular underlining of the privilege of living after the coming of Christ. The coming is new news, but the Son is not new. It was through Him that God created everything; He is the heir, He holds everything together. In fact, He is the perfect representation of the Father's nature. But there's more, that same Son has done the necessary work to pay for sin and is now seated at the Father's right hand. Consequently, He is greater than everyone, even the angels. So the rest of chapter 1 offers a chain of quotes to underline the fact that the Son is greater than any angel.

TRANSITION AND EXHORTATION: LISTEN TO HIM! (2:1-4)

Since people used to get in trouble when they neglected angel-borne messages, how much more should we be listening carefully to the message that the Lord Himself

---

1.   I am indebted to Craig Koester for this outline of Hebrews, as presented in his commentary, *Hebrews: Anchor Bible* vol. 36, (London: Doubleday, 2001).

has brought to us, and that we have seen confirmed by the working of the Spirit?

BIG IDEA (BASED ON PSALM 8): GOD WILL GLORIFY HUMANITY, JESUS PROVES IT! (2:5-9)

As great as angels are, God's great plan is to glorify humanity, the pinnacle of His creation. Even though we are by nature unimpressive (compared to angels), God's intent is for us to be the rulers of His great creation. But at this point in time, we don't see that plan fulfilled. So how can we have any confidence in God? Well, because we do see Jesus. He joined us in being a little lower than the angels, and He has gone on beyond death (which He died for everyone else) to now be crowned with glory and honour. So we can have confidence in God's plan for us, because of all that God has done already in the incarnational journey of His Son! Jesus came, Jesus died, Jesus rose and Jesus is glorified... and we get to play follow my leader!

The preacher now moves into the first of his three big movements in the message, each of which offers encouragement to us from the incarnation.

MOVEMENT 1 (BASED ON PSALM 95:7-11): PRESS ON INTO THE REST (2:10-5:10)

Amazingly, the Son of God came into the world and learned by suffering. He has been where we are, and He has felt it, and so He is not ashamed to call us His brothers. More than that, He is able to help us when we struggle with temptation.

So the preacher looks back to the wilderness generation under Moses. Jesus is greater than Moses, so we should trust Jesus more than they trusted Moses. He pulls in the warning of Psalm 95:7-11, repeatedly warning his hearers, just as the reader of the Psalm is urged to not be like that wilderness generation who missed out through a lack of faith and hardness of heart. The opportunity to enter into all that God intended, as symbolised by the idea of rest, is still before us and we can either trust Christ or be hard-hearted and unbelieving.

What difference does the incarnation make? Well, the end of chapter 4 tells us. We have a great high priest who has gone on ahead, but who first came to us and can fully sympathise with our weaknesses. We can have great confidence in approaching the throne of grace, precisely because the Son came to us first, experienced our life, prayed and trusted, and has gone on ahead of us!

Before the message moves into the second movement, picking up the Melchizedek hint introduced at the end of this section, the preacher first offers an exhortational transition again.

TRANSITION AND EXHORTATION: DON'T GO BACK! (5:11-6:20)

The recipients of the written sermon should have been mature, but they were immature. In fact, some in the group probably were not even saved. Facing pressure from increasing persecution, they were tempted to move backwards into the safety of synagogue Judaism. But this backwards move was not an option to consider; they should press on, not retreat. And how could they be certain of God's promise? Because Jesus has gone on ahead, into the heavenly temple, and is like an anchor there for His followers to pull on the rope and follow in that direction, not move the opposite way!

MOVEMENT 2 (BASED ON PSALM 110:4): PRESS ON INTO THE PRESENCE OF GOD (7:1-10:25)

This middle movement can feel slightly muddy for us today. Here the preacher presents Melchizedek and ties Jesus into him. How does that work? Well, Melchizedek was a mysterious character who only appears briefly in the story of Abraham (Gen. 14). But then Psalm 110 points to the messianic ruler being a priest in the order of Melchizedek. So the preacher to the Hebrews goes to town on the notion!

Melchizedek just seems to enter into human history, without having a full and normal pre-history (i.e. we don't know his origins). In a sense Jesus is similar. And since Melchizedek just fades back into the mists of time, we never think of him dying. Jesus is similar in that He won't die again! So in contrast to the priesthood of the Levites, this is an entirely better order of priesthood. After all, the old order could never deal with sin, but this better hope allows us to draw near to God.

Not only is it a better priesthood (ch. 7), Jesus gives us a better covenant (ch. 8). Jesus, after all, is the mediator of the New Covenant, which is entirely better than the old one and so replaced it. Jeremiah 31 is quoted to critique the old covenant and the rest of the section goes back and forth between critiquing the old and extolling the new covenant arrangement. So Jesus also went into a better sanctuary (ch. 9) with a better sacrifice (ch. 10).

In the old days, access into the holy of holies, the earthly picture of the heavenly throne room, was very restricted. But now Jesus has made a forever access for us into the real heavenly throne room. What is the relevance of the incarnation? He needed to be human to be able to shed the blood needed to create our access route. And that blood was the better sacrifice – not the temporary covering of animal blood, but the perfect sacrifice of His body for us, perfectly pleasing to God. Consequently believers can confidently and boldly march into the presence of God, fully assured in our hearts that we are welcome. The preacher wants us to press on into the presence of God, all because of what Jesus, our great high priest, has done for us.

TRANSITION AND EXHORTATION: DON'T TRAMPLE CHRIST! (10:26-39)

In light of who Christ is and what He has done, the preacher urges the recipients not to treat God's gift as worthless by giving in to the pressure of persecution. Instead they should keep their confidence and not shrink back but press on in faith. Here the preacher introduces the text for the final movement – Habakkuk 2:3-4 – which speaks of the just living by faith.

MOVEMENT 3 (BASED ON HABAKKUK 2:3-4): PRESS ON TOWARD YOUR REWARD! (11:1-12:24)

The great faith chapter might seem to have little to do with the Incarnate Christ. Not so. Hebrews 11 is really an extended introduction to the first verses of chapter 12. Faith is not the force that moves God, it is that which moves us to act on our trust in God, even when what we see does not offer supporting evidence. So the great hall of faith walks through the exploits of some great men and women of the Old Testament. The centrepiece is found in verses 13-16, where the 'by faith' pattern is broken and our eyes are drawn to Abraham's trust to the point of death without seeing what he hoped for, the reward, the city God is building, the hometown community of God's people. He hailed it from a distance, but he died still anticipating that ultimate repatriation.

So when we get to the end of the chapter we find that these great heroes, of whom the world was not worthy, died and are still waiting for us to receive the promised reward together with them. That is the great cloud of witnesses, testimonies to God's faithfulness in the toughest of times. And we are in the stadium running our race, aware of the witnesses, but looking to Jesus. There He is! The One who came to us and the One who ran the race first and has gone on ahead! He suffered, He pressed on, He anticipated the community of joy before Him and He did not shrink back.

The incarnate Christ is our motivation to press on when we are tempted to grow weary and give up. Our struggle is not as intense as His was. In fact, our very struggle is affirmation that God loves us because He disciplines those He loves. So the preacher urges the readers to consider their destiny. It is not Mount Sinai with all that was inadequate about the Old Covenant – that was a fearful place. But instead our destiny is Mount Zion and the city of God – a place of gathering to God the Father and His Son, a place of light and a place of community celebration! Indeed, a place where the incarnate Christ has gone on ahead of us.

TRANSITION AND EXHORTATION: DON'T REFUSE THE SPEAKING GOD! (12:25-27)

Again, they are urged to listen and not pull away from this communicating God.

CONCLUSION: LIVING IN LIGHT OF THE UNSHAKEABLE KINGDOM (12:28-13:21)

The themes of the book converge in the final section as the preacher urges the readers to serve God, to serve each other and to pay attention to their leaders. At the centre of this final section comes the reminder that Jesus does not change. In fact, the readers are urged to follow Him 'outside the gate' to the ignominy of His hideous death, for He has suffered to bring us to a better altar, even to the better and lasting city to come. The whole focus of the Christian life is to be on Christ: the One who became lower than angels in the incarnation, so that He could lead the way for us who follow Him back up to the rest, to the throne room of the heavenly temple, to the joyous city that will last forever!

*The reason the Son of God appeared was to destroy
the works of the devil.*
– 1 John 3:8b –

*It was just as though he had said, 'The first man
sinned by falling into disobedience; he paid no attention
to the command which had been given. ... But you
have established me as a second beginning for those
on earth, and I have been named a second Adam. In
me you see human nature purified, established sinless,
holy and pure. From now on bestow the good things of
your mercy, loose despair, rebuke corruption, and put an
end to the effects of your wrath. I have conquered even
Satan, the ancient ruler, for he found in me absolutely
nothing of his own.'[1]*

– Cyril of Alexandria, *On the Unity of Christ* –

*There was enmity between Christ and Satan, for
he came to destroy the works of the devil and to
deliver those who are under bondage to him. For that
purpose was he born; for that purpose did he live; for
that purpose did he die; for that purpose he has gone
into the glory, and for that purpose he will come
again, that everywhere he may find out his adversary
and utterly destroy him and his works from amongst
the sons of men.[2]*
– C.H. Spurgeon –

---

1. Cyril of Alexandria, '*On the Unity of Christ*', Sources Chrétiennes 97:444, quoted in Ancient Christian Commentary on Scripture, Vol. 10., Hebrews 5:7-10, p. 75.

2. C.H. Spurgeon, *Sermons*, 1326.664.

23

1 John:
Darkness Destroyed!

After all the millennia of messianic expectation offered in the Old Testament, it might be assumed that Jesus' arrival would be a source of ongoing celebration. It wasn't. The early church soon faced attacks from within on the doctrine of the incarnation itself.

GNOSTICISM, IF YOU KNOW WHAT I MEAN?

As the decades passed, early forms of the Gnostic heresy started to creep into the church and create significant problems. It would not be wise to project back later developed Gnosticism onto the church of the first century, but early hints and forms can be seen in the critique of several of the epistles.

Here's a super simplified summary of the situation. Under the influence of Greek thought, some people were buying into the notion that spirit is good and matter is bad. The great goal would therefore be to connect one's spirit with 'Spirit' itself – this greater reality. Access to that higher plane was reserved for those in the know (*gnosis* means knowledge). So having the secret knowledge was key to being on the inside of this elite crowd. There are nuances needed all over this explanation, but essentially this was the deal with Gnosticism.

This kind of secret handshake with the realm of 'Spirit' tended to lead in two directions for participants. If 'Spirit' is good, but matter is evil, then does matter really matter?

Some would tend toward the idea that the physical and material part of things needed to be suppressed and controlled. This would lead to asceticism where the individual would beat their body to bring it into subjection (we see hints of this in the Colossian version of the heresy, cf. Col. 2:20-23 or 1 Cor. 7:5).

But things could swing the other way too. If the body doesn't matter, then perhaps it was fine to sin, since the only realm that mattered was the spiritual realm. (We see this in 1 Cor. 6:12-20, and behind the situation that prompted 1 John.)

This view of spirit versus matter also led to one big issue with the coming of Christ. How could the Christ take on flesh? Surely He could not? With Gnostic ideas spreading, Christmas was under attack! The human Jesus surely could not be the Christ. Perhaps the Christ indwelt physical Jesus for a while, but he must have evaporated out at some point.

KNOWING GOD IS MORE THAN GNOSTICS COULD EVER KNOW!

The first epistle of John was written by the elder statesman apostle near the end of the first century. Some suggest that it was a circular letter to all the churches in an area, but there are clues that suggest it was written to a particular group of believers. They were caught up in the pain of a church split. It seems that some who had been part of the local church had turned out to be false teachers in some sort of Gnostic garb and they had moved out. Having left, they were now applying pressure to those that remained.

So the elderly apostle wrote his first epistle to the believers who were left in the church and suffering for their 'lack of knowledge'. He wrote to clarify the issue of sin and to underline the importance of the defining and distinguishing characteristic of true Christianity: love for one another. He wrote to help them discern that the Gnostic folks didn't have a secret something, but that they were missing the glorious experience of true Christianity: fellowship with the Trinity! And he wrote to reinforce the great news from a century earlier – that God's Son had taken on flesh and become one of us!

The letter launches with a direct critique of the lie that since Jesus was human (and therefore had a body), He had to be somehow distinguished from the 'spiritual' Christ. Perhaps John paused as he wrote of hearing and seeing and touching Christ. Three years of being with Christ remembered fondly for over six decades. That really was living, being with God in the flesh!

But it was not just a memory. John wrote to the Christians because he wanted them to know what he now experienced: an ongoing fellowship with God the Father and His Son, Jesus Christ.

He goes on for the rest of the first chapter to address some of the false claims of the Gnostic group. Their so-called fellowship with God was characterised by darkness.

Their faulty view of reality meant that they didn't view sin as sin and claimed to be sinless. However God is not about living in darkness, but light.

Here is the irony: the ones who had gone out were claiming to 'know God', but their lives did not demonstrate that they knew God. The contrast was like night and day. Instead of loving God and loving each other, these people loved the things of the world. Their spiritual claims were bold, but the reality seemed much more sinister.

In their denial of the incarnation they were cutting themselves off from the truth of Christ, and from knowing the Father. They may have had a 'secret knowledge', but it was not the kind of knowing that stirred the aged apostle's heart. They may have known something of darkness, but they didn't know the privilege of fellowship with the Trinity.

In contrast, the Christians to whom John wrote were anointed and so didn't need some sort of special teacher or teaching. So what were they to do? Abide in Christ.

Abide is relational language. Remain, stay in, dwell. The Christian life should not seem to be a frantic pursuit of something out of reach. Rather it should be an ongoing growth of personal knowledge of One who is known, a relationship with a God who gives Himself that we might enjoy fellowship with Him, in His Son, by His Spirit.

DARKNESS DESTROYED

One of the problems with church is that astonishing language can become so familiar. How many thousands of people have prayed repeatedly, 'Our Father, which art in...' Hold on a moment; our Father? What sort of language is that?

Actually, children who are blessed to have a good earthly father tend not to realise the privilege until later in life.

Perhaps they see the broken homes of their friends, or hear the stories of angry dads, or drunk dads, or absent dads, or abusive dads. Only then does the privilege of a loving father tend to sink in.

Perhaps Christians could do with exposure to the alternatives out there. What gods are there that are like our Father? Angry gods, self-absorbed gods, distant gods, even abusive gods... a quick open-top bus tour of the religious neighbourhood should bring us back to the God of the Bible with renewed appreciation.

'See what kind of love the Father has given to us, that we should be called children of God; and so we are' (1 John 3:1). The world does not have a clue, because they simply don't know Him (and that would include the false folks who claimed to be 'in the know'!).

How is it possible that we, sinners worthy of judgment, can become children of God? It is only possible because God is so loving that He sent His Son so that we would not need to perish. In that other great new birth passage, John 3, Jesus underlines that new birth is something from above, we receive it by God's goodness and by His Spirit and by simple trust in the provision of the One who became flesh so that He could be lifted up like the snake in the wilderness.

Jesus had pointed Nicodemus back to the serpent in the wilderness incident in Numbers 21:6-9. The premise was simple: don't strive for rescue, just look and live. Believing for salvation, what we tend to call faith, is about the gaze of our souls on the person of Christ.

Here in 1 John 3:1-3 John again returns to the importance of the gaze. Our relationship with God is not about our working for it. If there is a mechanism involved, it is our seeing Jesus for who He is and being transformed as a result. And one day we will see Him completely and clearly without any confusion or distraction. And then the transformation will be full and complete! So we are children now, and yet there is that to look forward to – what a hope!

To put it another way, we don't work our way into being a child of God. Childhood simply doesn't work that way. You can't earn child status: you are given it. By adoption or by birth, to be a child is not something you earn.

So the coming of Jesus made it possible for sinners in a dark sinful world to be brought into the light of fellowship with God. Everything the devil stands for is in opposition to this. The devil wants darkness, not light. The devil wants sin, not righteousness. The devil wants the lie, not the truth. The devil wants to keep people away from the joy of fellowship with God.

'The reason the Son of God appeared was to destroy the works of the devil!'

PATERNITY TESTS: LEGAL, GENETIC AND AMATEUR

Sadly the issue of paternity testing has become a greater feature of contemporary society. Spiritually speaking, this has always been a vital issue. Essentially there are three types of paternity tests:

1. The legal paternity test. This is where you take a birth certificate, or an adoption certificate, and match up the name of the father with a passport or other identification. Legal proof of being the father.

2. The genetic paternity test. This is where something in the DNA of the child matches the DNA of the father – there is something of him in the child. Genetic proof.

3. The amateur paternity test. This happens regularly – I'm sure you've practiced it. You see a child and with a laugh declare that no paternity test is necessary, the world can see the likeness to their dad!

The Bible points to all three. In Romans 8 and Galatians 4 we get to read of the privilege of adoption. We have been made children of God. But it is not just a legal issue. So often the gospel is presented in merely judicial or forensic terms. It is as if God has found a legal loophole and we have been given a mechanism by which we can do a deal with a distant God and so have special legal standing. But even the adoption passages push beyond a mere legal standing. In adoption we receive the Spirit of adoption so that our hearts cry out, 'Abba!'

Here in 1 John the apostle points to the other two tests. Right after the declaration of the incarnational mission to destroy the works of the devil, we read of God's seed abiding in the one who has been born of God. The word of Christ, by the Spirit, is like divine DNA in the life of the believer. And as with DNA, the result should be the amateur look-a-like paternity test. As those being transformed by God from the inside-out, it becomes evident which family we are in by our practice of righteousness, and by our love for one another. We share in the defining and distinctive characteristic of the God who is love; we start to resemble our Father!

No one has ever seen God;
the only God, who is at the Father's side,
he has made him known.
– John 1:18 –

This expression, however, 'the Word was made flesh',
can mean nothing else but that he partook of flesh
and blood like to us; he made our body his own, and
came forth man from a woman, not casting off his
existence as God, or his generation of God the Father,
but even in taking to himself flesh remaining what he
was. This the declaration of the correct faith proclaims
everywhere.[1]
– Cyril of Alexandria –

God did not degrade Himself by this condescension.
He did not in any sense make Himself to be less
than God. He remained God, and everything else
remained not God; the gulf still existed, even after
Jesus Christ had become man and had dwelt among
us. So instead of God degrading Himself when He
became man, He, by the act of Incarnation, elevated
mankind to Himself.[2]
– A. W. Tozer, *And He Dwelt Among Us* –

---

1.   Cyril of Alexandria, *Second Letter to Nestorius.*
2.   A. W. Tozer, *And He Dwelt Among Us (Ventura:* Regal, 2009), p. 72.

24

John:
God Made Known!

John's Gospel tends to get shelved at Christmas. Matthew gives us wise men and a foolish king. Luke gives us songs and shepherds. But John just goes back to the beginning and speaks of God, and His Word who is at His side. John's Gospel seems a long way from Bethlehem and the incarnation. Yet nothing could be further from the truth.

Perhaps John's prologue is the incarnation passage par excellence!

THE GLORIOUS GLIMPSE
Before there was anything, what was there? This is a great question. Somehow, if we can conceive of reality without

everything that has been created, perhaps we can get to the heart of what everything is really all about. Creation is wonderful, but a fallen creation is profoundly distracting and we struggle to keep our gaze on the central reality: God Himself.

So dare to strip away all that exists: people and places and problems... what is left? God. And what is He doing? Later in John's Gospel, in 17:24, Jesus gives us a glorious glimpse into the eternal experience of God. Is God pondering what commands to issue to a hypothetical future creation? Is God dwelling on His own sovereignty over all that might exist if He were to create? Actually, John's Gospel does not suggest a needy God who requires a creation to adjudicate or a realm to rule. The God we meet here is not a needy power-broker, but a loving self-giver.

Jesus is praying to His Father for those who would believe in Him based on the word of the apostles. To put that another way, He is praying for us. He is praying and desiring that we should one day be with Him to see the glory that the Father has given to the Son. Is this Jesus praying selfishly that we would get to see how special He is? Not at all. It is actually that He wants us to see what kind of Father His Father is: a loving giver of glory!

When humanity manufactures a god in our own image, we always end up with a needy super-being who is a self-absorbed power-broker, a glory-grabbing god, if you will. We need to stop and check this default deity description against Scripture. Perhaps we are projecting our fallen image onto a God who is nothing like that!

So what was God doing before anything else existed? He was loving and glorifying. He was sharing and praising. He was celebrating the Other in the perfection of divine fellowship!

In John 17 we read of the lovingly glorious relationship between the Father and Son. And we catch a glimpse of that reality right at the beginning of the gospel.

IN THE BEGINNING

In the beginning there was God. And with God was the Word, who was God. One God. Confusing? Sure. How can there be two 'Gods' who are with each other and yet both be God? Hold on to that question.

At the same time as pondering the complexities of God and His Word, don't miss what is being presented right up front here. God is a communicator, otherwise why all this talk of the Word? And what is to be found in that Word? Life and light. God is a communicating, life-giving, shining-out kind of God. This is no self-absorbed black hole sucking glory from all that exists; if anything the arrows need to go in the other direction – communication to us, life to us, light to us.

So John goes on to describe the coming of the messenger, also called John. This one, the Baptist, came to point people to the light. And the Baptist's timing was perfect (obviously, since God sent him), for the light was coming into the world!

It reads as if the Word of God came into the world under cover. 'He was in the world, and the world was made through him, yet the world did not know him. He came to his own, and his own people did not receive him' (1:10). Here was the Creator Himself, coming to His own people, and being rejected. Astonishing.

At the same time, there were some who did receive Him – which means to believe in who He was, trusting Him to be their Saviour. These people received the greatest privilege – the right to become children of God!

So John's prologue reaches its conclusion with five verses that bring this phenomenal section to a fitting climax. In verses 14-18 John explains how the Word came into creation under cover. He explains how there can be two LORDS, yet only one God. And in just five words he invites us into the greatest privilege humanity could ever have.

UNDER COVER

So far what has been presented of this One called the Word is highly impressive: He is with God, He is God, He made everything, He possesses life, He offers light, He defeats darkness, He has come into the world, He has been rejected by His own, He has given family rights to those who believed in Him.

But the question remains, how did He come to His own? Did He come in an angelic chariot, or an awesome vision, or as a super-being made manifest? John launches this paragraph with a stunning statement: He became flesh and dwelt amongst us.

He became flesh? That is remarkable. He chose to step into humanity in order to come to us. That really is coming all the way in our direction. He chose to become one of us. After all the passages that we have considered together, this might seem like old news, but it should still give us pause for thought.

He became flesh and dwelt among us. He came to live where we live. He came to our kind of life. Not the palace of Herod kind of life, but the Nowhere-Nazareth, in Galilee, kind of life. And as the older versions of the Bible put it, he 'tabernacled' amongst us, which is to say, He pitched His tent down here where we are.

TWO LORDS OR ONE?

He pitched His tent, and we have seen His glory, full of grace and truth? This should sound familiar. John is pointing back to that key moment in Exodus that we considered in the chapter on Moses the Prophet.

Moses was with the LORD on the mountain, away from the people, and the LORD was angry. Bizarrely, Moses then asks to see God's glory. Somehow in his negotiations with an angry jilted husband God, he dares to ask to see God's glory. Amazingly the LORD responds favourably. Glory? Yes. Face? No.

It turns out that both in the description of the glory encounter (Exod. 33:18-23) and the actual display moment (34:5-8) God declares descriptions of His goodness and kindness. It is not the power show we tend to expect as we read it, but a powerful presentation of God's heart.

Moses did not get to see the face of the LORD, but he did get an awesome encounter with a God of grace. So how is it that he had the confidence to ask for this special moment?

Just a few verses earlier in Exodus 33:7-11 we read of Moses' normal practice. He would regularly head out to the tent of meeting, which was pitched on the level of the people. There he would meet the LORD face to face, as a man speaks with his friend. Somehow it was his knowledge of the LORD who pitches His tent down near the people that gave him the confidence to ask for a glimpse of the glory of the unseen LORD up on the mountain.

The God who Moses met with on the mountain was One who could speak of 'all my goodness' and of being gracious and of showing mercy. This God was slow to anger and steadfastly loving and forgiving. This God abounded in steadfast love and faithfulness. He was not to be taken lightly for He would judge, seemingly in the context of this overwhelming love.

He abounded in steadfast love and faithfulness. This is that wondrous Old Testament pairing of God's loyal love and His remaining true. This is God's loyal loving loyalty, His true gracious true-ness. To put it in New Testament terms, this is the God who is full of grace and truth.

So the mystery of the two LORDS in Exodus 33 is revealed. Moses met with the God who reveals God. He met regularly with the Word who pitches His tent amongst us and whose glory can be seen. This 'became flesh' God is the communication of the Father at whose side He has always been. Just as in Moses' day, Moses may have been the one who carried the Law to the people, but the steadfast love and faithfulness of the LORD on the mountain were first conveyed through the LORD in the tent of meeting.

GOD REVEALED
No-one has ever seen God. These are striking words. God the Father is God invisible. Sounds profoundly disappointing. However, the only God, who is at the Father's side, He has done something profoundly wonderful for us. Here come the five words that offer us the greatest privilege of all:

HE HAS MADE HIM KNOWN
Surely this is the right place to finish a book on the Incarnation. As Jesus would put it in a later conversation, 'if you have seen me, you have seen the Father' (14:7). The desire of the disciple in the upper room (John 14:8-9) is the deepest need of every human. If only we could see the God who made us, the God who created so generously

and is in charge and gives meaning to everything. If only we could know Him – but we are mere humans, we are just creatures in a vast creation. There is no way that we can know Him.

There is no way, that is, unless He should choose to come to us, and become one of us, and He did. The only God, who is at the Father's side, He took on flesh and pitched His tent among us. He has let us all see His glory, which means we have been able to receive grace upon grace. The truly gracious true-ness of God, His loyal loving loyalty, it is ours in the Son!

The Son has always been the communication of the Father toward us, but in the Incarnation we have a moment in time where He became flesh and pitched His tent among us. And He invites us into His Word to meet with Him face to face, as a man meets with His friend. And as we come to Him, the Son, we get to see the Father made known to us.

The incarnation is an invitation, an invitation to know the Father, in the Son – a truly good God whose eternal communion is now offered to us in the Son, by the Spirit. At the centre of the universe there is a glory-giving, loving relationship, and in the incarnation we are invited to join in!

Conclusion

Great indeed, we confess, is the mystery of godliness:
He was manifested in the flesh ...
- 1 Timothy 3:16 -

In one of Paul's final letters he sent a host of practical instruction to Timothy, his representative in Ephesus. He was concerned that the church there should know how to live out the Christian life. Suddenly he breaks from the practical instructions concerning men and women, elders and deacons, and makes a bold statement quoting an early Christian hymn.

There was a unanimous agreement among early Christians concerning the mystery of godliness. This mystery was in some way veiled or hidden, but had now been made known in the times of the New Testament. Pause there. Are we saying that the people who claimed to know God in the Old Testament somehow failed to achieve God-pleasing godliness? Yes, that is exactly what we are saying! But then came the New Testament, and the secret was revealed.

This is exciting stuff! What is the revealed secret of true godliness? Is it a new discipline, or a certain type of resolution, or a greater commitment to church attendance, or a radical lifestyle change, or what? What can we do to achieve this godliness which we all know is lacking in ourselves?

Wrong question. It's that Genesis 3 question again, with the hiss still present. What can *I* do to be considered good independently of any true union with God? Nothing. Paul says the mystery, the now revealed secret of godliness, is 'He!'

The right question is not 'what?' but 'who?' And the who is not you or me, it is Him. The secret to godliness, and Christianity, and true religion, and pleasing God, and living the faith is simple, it is Him! He, who?

For the next six lines, Paul quotes this hymn that assumes Christ to be the subject of every line. And where does it begin? It begins with the incarnation. *He was manifested in the flesh.*

It has to begin there, doesn't it? If what God wants from us is not our independent righteousness but rather truly united relationship with the Son, then the revealed secret of godliness has to begin with Christmas. Instructions could have been sent in other ways. But heart-capturing self-revelation had to be done in the flesh. Sometimes a letter just won't do. Sometimes even a voice message is not enough. Sometimes it just has to be face to face.

He was manifest in the flesh. He did not come as a coach, intent on helping us function more effectively. He did not come as a police officer, intent on helping us function within the bounds of the law. He did not come as a lecturer, intent on informing us of that which we need to live successfully. He came as a groom intent on wooing a bride. Anything less could never achieve the goal of godliness. Once wooed and captured, our heartfelt response would far exceed any self-determined commitment to self-transformation.

The need on our side was deathly desperate, and the love on God's side was abundantly overflowing. So He was manifest in the flesh. The forever focus of the Father's delight was sent to earth for us. He became flesh and dwelt among us. He revealed God the Father to us. He came to rescue and woo us. And now we can enter into that delightful communion that is our Triune God. We can know the Father, revealed to us by the Son. We can know the fellowship of the Father and Son, by the Spirit purchased for us by the Son. It is not about you. It is not about me. It is all about Him. And in the Incarnation, He came to us!

> Veiled in flesh the Godhead see,
> Hail the incarnate deity,
> Pleased as man with man to dwell,
> Jesus our Immanuel!

Sources Cited

Augustine, *City of God*.

_____, *Sermons* 191.1.

Bainton, Roland. *Here I Stand: A Life of Martin Luther.* New York: Abingdon Cokesbury, 1950.

Bock, Darrell. *Luke: Baker Exegetical Commentary on the New Testament.* Grand Rapids: Baker, 1994.

Calvin, John. *Institutes of the Christian Religion*, McNeil ed. London: Westminster, 1960

Chesterton, G.K. *Orthodoxy*. Los Angeles: John Lane Company, 1909.

Cyril of Alexandria, *Commentary on Luke, Homily 73.*

_____. 'On the Unity of Christ', Sources Chrétiennes 97:444, quoted in Heen, Erik and Philip Krey. *Ancient Christian Commentary on Scripture,* Vol. 10. IVP, 2005.

_____. *Second Letter to Nestorius.*

Edwards, Jonathan. *A History of the Work of Redemption,* in *The Works of Jonathan Edwards,* Vol. 9. Yale, 1989.

Gregory of Nazianzus, *Orations* XXIX.19.

Kaiser, Walter. *The Promise Plan of God.* Grand Rapids: Zondervan, 2008.

Koester, Craig. *Hebrews: A New Translation with Introduction and Commentary.* The Anchor Bible, vol. 36. Doubleday, 2001.

Luther, Martin. *On the Councils and the Church,* in Luther's Works vol. 41.

Maier, Paul. *In the Fullness of Time: A Historian Looks at Christmas, Easter and the Early Church.* Grand Rapids: Kregel, 1977.

Packer, J.I. *Knowing God.* IVP, 1973.

Pusey, P.E., *Cyril of Alexandria.* Oxford, 1868-77.

Scougal, Henry. *The Life of God in the Soul of Man.* Boston, 1868.

Seuss, Dr. *How the Grinch Stole Christmas.* New York: Random House, 1957.

Smith, Wilbur M. *The Supernaturalness of Christ.* 2011.

Spurgeon, C.H. *Sermons.*

Tozer, A.W. *And He Dwelt Among Us. Ventura: Regal, 2009.*

Warfield, Benjamin B. *Selected Shorter Writings*, Vol. 1. Minnesota: Presbyterian & Reformed, 1970.

HYMNS

Card, Michael. 'Immanuel', The Promise. CD. 1991.

Lowry, Mark. 'Mary Did You Know?' Hymn, 1984.

Spafford, Horatio. 'When Peace Like a River', Hymn, 1874.

Townend, Stuart. 'Immanuel', Hymn, 1999.

Wade, John F. 'O Come All Ye Faithful', Hymn, ca. 1743

Wesley, Charles. 'Hark the Herald Angels Sing', Hymn, 1739.

MAGNIFICENT
OBSESSION
WHY JESUS *IS* GREAT
DAVID ROBERTSON

ISBN 978-1-78191-271-3

Magnificent Obsession
DAVID ROBERTSON

David Robertson, author of *The Dawkins Letters*, was told by the leader of an atheist society: "Okay, I admit that you have destroyed my atheism, but what do you believe?" His answer was "I believe in and because of Jesus." This book shows us why Jesus is the reason to believe. In response to the shout of "God is not Great" by the late Christopher Hitchens, David shows us why Jesus is God and is Great.

Engaging and insightful... This book is useful no matter what your experience and where you stand on matters of faith.

Tim Keller

Senior Pastor, Redeemer Presbyterian Church, New York City, New York

We will share this "Magnificent Obsession" so that ... friends may discover not only what it means but why it matters.

Alistair Begg

Senior Pastor, Parkside Church, Chagrin Falls, Ohio

David and I disagree on a great many things, but we are unified understanding the importance of this ongoing debate.

Gary McLelland

Atheist, blogger and secular campaigner, Edinburgh, Scotland

I love this book! It's an excellent, conversational introduction to Christianity for non-Christians and new Christians who are wrestling with questions.

Jon Bloom

President, Desiring God, Minneapolis, Minnesota

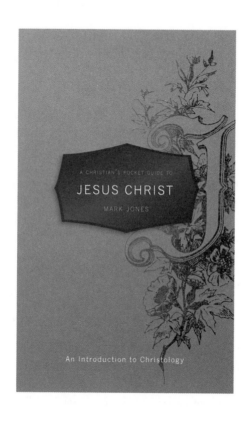

A CHRISTIAN'S POCKET GUIDE TO

JESUS CHRIST

MARK JONES

An Introduction to Christology

ISBN 978-1-84550-951-4

A Christian's Pocket Guide to Jesus Christ

MARK JONES

Through this book we get to know the Son of God who indeed is God and not just a superman! He is the one who came from above and became fully human having a human body and soul. Being God enabled him to pay the debt owed for sin and being man enabled him to stand on man's behalf for their sin. In straightforward and simple layman terms this book will explain the interconnectivity of the work and person of Jesus Christ and dispel any misconceptions you may have.

Mark Jones is the Minister of Faith Reformed Presbyterian Church (PCA), Vancouver, Canada. He is married to Barbara and they have four children.

Mark Jones has served us well by writing this short introduction to the doctrine of Christ. His book is biblical, clear, and rooted in historic Reformed theology.

Joel R. Beeke

President and Professor of Systematic Theology and Homiletics,
Puritan Reformed Theological Seminary, Grand Rapids, Michigan

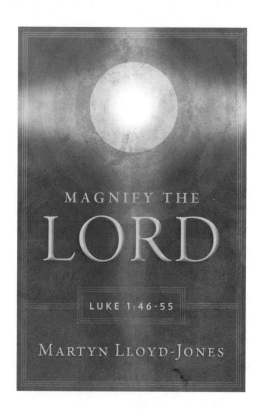

MAGNIFY THE
LORD

LUKE 1:46-55

MARTYN LLOYD-JONES

ISBN 978-1-84550-754-1

Magnify the Lord
MARTYN LLOYD-JONES

Introduced by Russell Moore. How do we respond to the sheer wonder of the incarnation of God's Son? Mary responded to the announcement of the birth of the Saviour with a song of praise. Her words were deep and with feeling - truly an experience which had affected her inner being. Yes, she was confused at first but she was willing to submit to God. She praises God for His character and for keeping His promises even when circumstances seemed to contradict that with the long wait over centuries for the Messiah. In this delightful book, co-published with Bryntirion Press, Martyn Lloyd-Jones meditates on Mary's Song of Praise and applies it to our lives. He looks at our response to God and how God deals with us. We find that the new birth is all of God and nothing of ourselves.

Martyn Lloyd-Jones (1899-1981) was born in Wales. He was a dairyman's assistant, a political enthusiast, debater, and chief clinical assistant to Sir Thomas Harder, the King's Physician. But at the age of 27 he gave up a most promising medical career to become a preacher. He had a far-reaching influence through his ministry at Westminster Chapel in London, England from 1938-68. His published works have had an unprecedented circulation, selling in millions of copies.

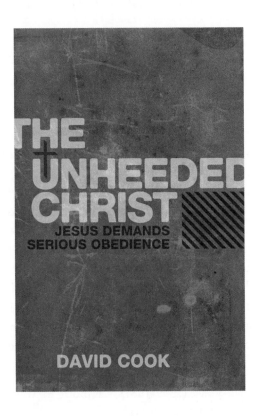

THE
UNHEEDED
CHRIST
JESUS DEMANDS
SERIOUS OBEDIENCE

DAVID COOK

ISBN 978-1-84550-369-7

The Unheeded Christ
DAVID COOK

Jesus Christ is a provocative, uncompromising teacher. Yet it is easy to become so accustomed to Jesus' words that they become old friends – comfortable, unfamiliar, unchallenging. We get so used to him that we forget to take notice of what he commands us to do. Jesus demands serious obedience from his people in all areas of life. Here he challenges us about crucial issues – loving enemies, forgiveness, sex, ambition, adultery, wealth accumulation, revenge, impending judgement, resolving tension between Christians and self-delusion.

His words come across as fresh, immediate, wise, authentic and discerning. Listen to him again – and this time, don't let him go unheeded.

David has recently retired from his role as Principal and Director of the School of Preaching at Sydney Missionary and Bible College (SMBC). He is now now involved in an itinerant preaching and teaching ministry, He is a Presbyterian minister and a graduate of SMBC and Moore Theological College. Prior to formal studies and pastoral ministry David worked in the Economic Research Department of the Reserve Bank. He has spoken at a number of Christian Conventions including Keswick.

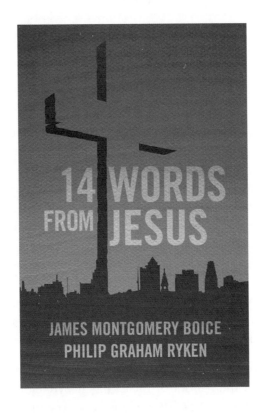

ISBN 978-1-78191-205-8

14 Words from Jesus
James Montgomery Boice, Philip G. Ryken

These inspirational readings probe Christ's seven words from the cross and equally significant, seven words from the risen Lord, after his death. These words highlight the glory of Calvary, the heart of God and how wonderfully Jesus understood that his death and resurrection was to be effective in bringing into being atonement from sin for those seeking forgiveness.

James Montgomery Boice (1938-2000) was pastor of Tenth Presbyterian Church, Philadelphia from 1968 until his death in 2000. He served as Chairman of the International Council on Biblical Inerrancy and was a founding member of the Alliance of Confessing Evangelicals. He was a prolific author and published over 50 works.

Philip G. Ryken became President of Wheaton College in July 2010. Prior to that he was Senior Minister of Tenth Presbyterian Church, Philadelphia, Pennsylvania. He is also a prolific author and a member of the council of The Gospel Coalition.

Boice and Ryken are both excellent preachers, but first and foremost they are writing as men who have themselves been transformed by the words of Jesus. Reading this book, his words will come to you freshly too and you cannot help but marvel at his saving and transforming work.

Adrian Reynolds
Director of Ministry, The Proclamation Trust & Associate Minister, East
London Tabernacle Baptist Church, London

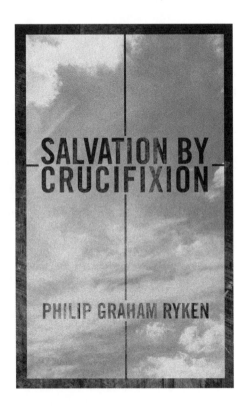

SALVATION BY
CRUCIFIXION

PHILIP GRAHAM RYKEN

ISBN 978-1-78191-307-9

Salvation by Crucifixion
PHILIP G. RYKEN

The author celebrates Easter with this thoughtful guidebook to understanding the cross. Seven answers to seven questions explain the why and the wherefore of the cross for a Biblical faith and a Christian life. Ryken covers the necessity of the cross for salvation; the offense it gives to Jews, Gentiles, and any moral individual; the peace it brings to those who trust in Christ; the power it has to achieve God's loving, saving purpose; the triumph it wins over sin, death, and the judgment of God; the humility it displays in the character of Jesus; and the boast it becomes for every believer.

Artful, but simple; compact, but loaded; sound, but fresh. This book is a jewel. Some passages sing. It well repays the time it takes to read it.

Mark Dever
Senior Pastor of Capitol Hill Baptist Church and President of 9Marks.org, Washington, DC

The cross is the center of the Christian life and message... But what does it mean? And how does that apply to our lives? This little book will help explain that to interested readers.

Josh Moody
Senior Pastor of College Church, Wheaton, Illinois

Christian Focus Publications

Our mission statement –

STAYING FAITHFUL
In dependence upon God we seek to impact the world through literature faithful to His infallible Word, the Bible. Our aim is to ensure that the Lord Jesus Christ is presented as the only hope to obtain forgiveness of sin, live a useful life and look forward to heaven with Him.

Our books are published in four imprints:

CHRISTIAN
FOCUS

Popular works including biographies, commentaries, basic doctrine and Christian living.

CHRISTIAN
HERITAGE

Books representing some of the best material from the rich heritage of the church.

MENTOR

Books written at a level suitable for Bible College and seminary students, pastors, and other serious readers. The imprint includes commentaries, doctrinal studies, examination of current issues and church history.

CF4•K

Children's books for quality Bible teaching and for all age groups: Sunday school curriculum, puzzle and activity books; personal and family devotional titles, biographies and inspirational stories – because you are never too young to know Jesus!

Christian Focus Publications Ltd,
Geanies House, Fearn, Ross-shire,
IV20 1TW, Scotland, United Kingdom.
www.christianfocus.com